Flowers and Festivals of the Jewish Year

Flowers and Festivals
of the
Jewish Year

by
LILLIAN S. FREEHOF
and
LOTTIE C. BANDMAN

Drawings and photographs by
S. William Hinzman
(except where otherwise noted
on page 186)

HEARTHSIDE PRESS, INCORPORATED
Publishers • *New York*

Dedicated to
Our Patient Husbands
Solomon B. Freehof
and
Chester G. Bandman
for their constant understanding,
sympathy and affectionate criticism.

Acknowledgments

Since the scope of this book was so wide, including the sanctuary as well as the home, it was necessary to call on the assistance of many friends and co-workers. We take this opportunity of thanking all of our contributors for their gracious and spontaneous cooperation. Our thanks go also to Mrs. Milton E. Harris for her encouragement in the early stage of our work. A grateful word to Reizenstein's Inc., Mrs. Samuel Allon, Mr. Lester Smith, Zentler Linen Shop and the Rodef Shalom Gift Corner for the loan of materials, and to the Pittsburgh Garden Center, to Phipps Conservatory with particular thanks to Mr. Frank S. Curto, its director. To the staff of Rodef Shalom Temple in Pittsburgh, a warm word of gratitude.

We express added appreciation to a few special people:

To Rae L. Goldson of Woodmere, New York, who gave the initial impetus; to Mrs. Malcolm J. Marks, for her invaluable assistance with the information on mechanics; and to Mrs. Jerome E. Markstein, for her equally valuable assistance with the material on drying flowers and foliage.

To our photographers:

Jonas Studio Inc. who worked so enthusiastically and artistically with us on our wedding pictures;

The Latent Image: Mr. Russell W. Streiner and Mr. George A. Romero, and particularly to Mr. S. William Hinzman we add an extra warm-hearted salute for his exceptional help with the diagrams, sketches, and drawings in the chapter, "The Science of Flower Arranging."

To Mrs. Nedda Anders, our publisher, who gave welcome and pertinent advice, and friendly encouragement.

Lillian S. Freehof and Lottie C. Bandman.

Contents

Foreword

Most of our Jewish festivals occur at the seasons of planting or harvesting. In our celebrations of these holidays we use the produce of the earth to enhance the mood of our religious expression. This inherited custom harmonizes with an important modern interest, that of flower arrangements and table-setting displays, which has grown to great proportions in recent years, so much so that even our gentlemen have formed garden clubs of their own.

Our purpose in providing this book of *Flowers and Festivals of the Jewish Year,* of floral arrangements, table-settings, synagogue and home decorations for the festivals, is to combine these historic and contemporary interests.

The plan of the book is simple. The chapters follow the order of the Jewish Year, starting in the autumn. Each chapter contains three parts. First we explain the idea and the spirit of the Sabbath and each festival so that the decorations will appropriately express the mood of the holiday. Second, we present photographs of floral arrangements and table displays, arrangements of fruits, symbols, and home decorations, and third, descriptions of the pictures.

Many people may wish to use these suggestions. Others, undoubtedly, will be inspired to create their own original arrangements. We hope this book will be a useful guide to beautifying our Jewish festivals in synagogue and home.

L.S.F and L.C.B.

CHAPTER ONE

Beautifying the Festivals

THE GARDEN OF LIFE

GOD was the world's first gardener. After He created the sun and the moon and the stars, the firmament and the dry land, the animals that roamed the earth and the fishes that plunged into the waters, He then created the Garden of Eden.

The Bible could have begun on some high mountaintop. It could have begun at an impressive seashore within sound of the thunderous surf. But God began it in a garden. There were trees in the ancient garden, fruit trees and shade trees. There were bushes and shrubs and flowers. It is surprising how botanical the Bible is in these two first chapters of sacred scripture. Clearly it wants to impress us 'with the idea that man's original happiness was in the setting of a garden among the natural beauties of growing nature. From this garden of nature we were never completely expelled. The growing splendor of the world has always maintained our life and sustained our spirit. Expanding scientific knowledge has only deepened our awareness of the blessings of earth's garden to the life of man. The winds change the air, the trees bear fruit or give shade and the very tiny insects in the earth convert the dead leaves and branches into fruitful

soil. The complex balance of nature surrounds us, sustains us. We are part of the garden of life.

When God created the first man and the first woman, He placed them in this garden. First came the garden and then the woman. First came beauty and then the appreciation of it. So we may fancifully assume that Eve may well have been the founder of the first garden club in the world.

Scripture does not hint at this, nor does the Midrash develop any such theme, but it is not a far step for the imagination to picture Eve, as she plucked the forbidden fruit, arranging a few leaves or blossoms. Thus beauty may have been introduced into the world as early as the blessing of food, and the sustenance for spiritual life was coincidental with the sustenance for physical life. Witness the fact that before the cherry tree puts forth its fruit it displays its creativeness by a beautiful blossoming. The fragrance of the bloom of the apple tree is as tempting as the fruit which follows.

THE FORBIDDEN FRUIT

The legend has come down through history that it was the apple of which Eve ate, and if that were true, was it the bloom of the tree which first attracted her? But, was it the apple? Every people in the world has made its own guess. Perhaps the wisest guess might be found in our own legendary material in the Midrash.

1. Elegant rubrum lilies and curled ti leaves form an impressive setting for the bronze figure of Verocchio's "David" placed in front of blond wood paneling in a library of rare Hebrew books. Because the soft dark pollen of this lily stains so readily, the florist usually removes the stamen as soon as the bud opens. To enjoy the full beauty of contrasting mahogany stamens against rich ivory petals, a collar of wax paper was placed around the stamen while the arrangement was being made. When finished the wax paper collar was carefully cut away. A soft wire was Scotch-taped to the back of the ti leaves to facilitate curling and bending the leaves. This composition was planned to celebrate the Jewish Book Festival. *Arranged by Mrs. J. Arthur Stein, Pittsburgh, Pa.*

2. In observance of Jewish Book Month, a floral decoration in the Lippmann Library of Rodef Shalom Temple features dark red celosia as a center of interest with feathery celosia, bells of Ireland and caladium leaves. *Arranged by Mrs. James H. Rich, Pittsburgh, Pa.*

The Midrash indicates that it was the fig of which Eve ate. After she had also betrayed Adam into eating the forbidden fruit and they were compelled to hide their "shame," they begged all the trees for leaves to cover them and only the fig tree would answer their plea. And the Rabbis say that the tree from which they sinned was also the tree from which they received their solace. But, whatever was the fruit, we like to think that very early in the creation of the world, the first woman must surely have been interested in fruit and flower arrangements.

THE LURE OF THE BLOSSOM

We do not attempt to follow that thin thread of artistic taste down through history to show the evolution and growth of the garden clubs of today and the interest in flower arrangements which have spread to such vast proportions in recent years. If we did, we might find that Mrs. Noah, in spite of the thousands of animals she had to care for, also was careful to save some plants by taking a flower or a shrub or two in the Ark. Perhaps that was why, when the Flood receded

3. For a Jewish art festival, a Moissaye Marans figure of Isaiah is combined with bold plant material. The terra cotta color in figure and flagstone base is echoed in red-edged green pandanus, brown dracaena, metallic echeveria, and gray and red begonia leaves. *Arranged by Mrs. David H. Green, White Plains, N. Y.*

and Noah and his family came out of the Ark, Noah was able to plant the vines which brought forth the grapes of wine.

Surely Sarah and Rebecca and Rachel, living in Palestine, where evergreen shrubs and lemon trees and hyacinths and tulips abounded, must have put the flowers and the trees and the shrubs to use for beautifying their own homes.

OUR AGRICULTURAL HERITAGE

All through biblical times the Jews were primarily an agricultural people. They ploughed their fields. They sowed their seeds. They reaped and they harvested. Their closeness to the life-giving earth gave them a sense of its beauty as well as its nourishment, and they turned naturally to the use of flowers as a means of decoration. At the Feast of Harvests the first crop of fruits was brought in baskets to Jerusalem to be offered on the altar. Crowning these gift-baskets were the choicest of flowers. The people marched in procession to the altar and leading this procession was the sacrificial animal with a wreath of olive on its head, its horns covered with gold.

Shabuoth, the festival day of the harvest, is designated as a judgment day of trees. One authority stated that it was customary to place trees in the synagogue, but another authority prohibits this because it is aping a gentile custom.

The rose was pre-eminent amongst the flowers. In praising his Shulamite heroine, Solomon compared her to "the rose of Sharon." The Mishnah calls this the "king's rose." Once it was the custom to scatter roses and other fragrant blossoms on the floor of the synagogue. In the Palestinian sanctuaries, flowers were distributed to the worshippers as they left the services on the Eve of Passover. And at the other festivals, the house and the synagogue were decorated with flowers.

4. This interesting composition, planned for the social hour which followed a Jewish music festival held in the temple, features two large red and yellow chrysanthemums and two buds. Leucothoe foliage, with red tips to match the flowers, partly conceals the two containers made of tin cans covered with sycamore bark (bamboo mats could be used). The accessory is a happy choice in carrying out the theme and the cork base harmonizes beautifully to complete the arrangement. *Arranged by Mrs. Rinehart J. Cleary, Pittsburgh, Pa.*

5. Children are always fascinated by interpretations of Bible stories. Here Noah's Ark became the container, with the animals as accessories, for a table decoration for a birthday party during *Chanuko*. The birds on the napkins and the chrysanthemums were orange and the gladioli were white; the striped zebras, blue cloth and the white napkins turned the whole into a magic of color. *Arranged by Mrs. Alan H. Azen, Pittsburgh, Pa.*

Jewish artists throughout the centuries have made lavish use of floral subjects in their art work. Forbidden to depict the human form by the commandment: "Thou shalt make no graven images," they turned to the field and the forest, the tree and the shrub, and the brightly colored flowers.

OUR MODERN PROMISE

And so down we come to our own day when interest in flowers and floral arrangements has become so absorbing a part of our life. Perhaps it is because we are far removed from the agricultural life that we try so hard to get back to nature. In the crowded cities we have worked diligently to counteract the steel and cement and dust which may move us along the road of progress but which banish the soft beauty of nature. So in every little garden plot we try to reconvert this world of iron and stone which has become our landscape back into the "paradise," the garden which came first out of the ancient chaos.

"EACH MAN SHALL SIT UNDER HIS OWN VINE AND FIG TREE." — (Micah IV, 4)

Our modern interest in landscaping, gardening and flower arranging seems to point towards the fulfillment of the pro-

6. The arrangement for this Sisterhood Donor dais was kept low so the speakers could be in full view. The focal point was a full, open artichoke seed head. Around it were okra pods, fern seed, spruce cones and eucalyptus bells with dried wheat, sea oats and cattails. White doves and candles, and colorful chrysanthemums gave needed contrast to the beige and brown monotones. This arrangement would be fine also for a *Bath Mitzvah* or *Rosh Hashonah* reception table, changing the flowers to suit the season. *Courtesy, Temple Beth Israel, Altoona, Pa. Arranged by Mrs. Martin Goodman, Hollidaysburg, Pa.*

phetic promise that each man should have his own "garden spot" in connection with his home. Even a few flowers and branches brought indoors contribute a sense of well-being and contentment to the home, whether it be large and luxurious, or small and modest. The purpose of the art and descriptions in this book is to stimulate interest in making the Jewish holidays more attractive in home observance particularly and to recapture in the mood of today the biblical tradition of bringing plants and flowers and fruits into the home as well as into the temple or synagogue for all celebrations.

Garden clubs and thoughtful flower arranging have captivated the interest of the modern woman. One need not be an expert in order to have pleasing decorations in her surroundings. From simple efforts and repeated experiments along with free use of the imagination, skill is readily attained, thus making it easier also to appreciate and enjoy the accomplishment of others.

Numerous up-to-date home and garden magazines as well as many fascinating current books on flower arrangements and table settings, provide the most challenging pictures, instructions and suggestions. The American woman's absorption in interior decorating and even in the art of painting has developed her aesthetic taste to a point beyond the rating of an amateur. This same interest may be applied to her study of design, scale, balance, color and harmony between container and flowers—until each achievement will bring new confidence and an added satisfaction in acquiring a stimulating hobby.

Flower arranging has become a serious art in itself. At present there is a strong trend toward oriental design. However, only the sophisticated in the art may attempt to work with abstract arrangements. Accessories or basic framework, such as driftwood, glass, steel and sculpture, have taken the place of masses of flowers. Fewer flowers and more accessories create today's pattern, except of course in a mass design.

7. This delightful table may well serve for a child's birthday table during a festival, in particular during *Purim*. The gay character of the setting needs only the familiar *Purim* symbols, the mask and the *homontaschen*, to complete the picture. *Courtesy of Beth Shalom Synagogue, Pittsburgh, Pa. Arranged by Mrs. Samuel Litvak, Mrs. Julius Kruman, Mrs. Max Joel.*

For years dried materials have held a prominent place in the program of the arranger. Today even the natural-looking permanent flowers have won approval because of their practicability.

The fascination of this floral art inspires novices to seek further knowledge and to acquire greater skill. Certain types of arrangements suit certain types of homes better than others. Nevertheless, the trend today approves the mixing of period, line and contemporary designs. So, too, do the best authorities combine many categories of fabrics, pictures and furniture in decorating. The present taste in arranging leans towards the more casual and less stylized, except for flower shows. Thus, especially in the home, one is freer in working with flowers and greens, fruits and vegetables, but at the same time is conscious of suitable lines, colors, textures, and proportions of the containers and plant materials for the surroundings in which they are to be placed.

8. A triangle of ti leaves, succulents and white button chrysanthemums in a white oval bowl makes a handsome, long-lasting arrangement for a holiday decoration. *Courtesy of Temple Emanu-El, San Francisco, Calif. Arranged by Mrs. Leonard M. Tivol.*

9. A touch of beauty in the home—whatever the season, whatever the occasion. This oriental dried arrangement consists of sable palm, dock, dried pale green hydrangea, and flowers of semi-precious stone petals on sterling silver stems. The composition in a cast iron usubata ox-cart is placed on a Japanese tree slab, to be used alone or to serve as the "conversation-piece" of a buffet table. *Arranged by Mrs. S. W. Herwald, Pittsburgh, Pa.*

Wherever the arrangement is made and whatever style is followed, the aim is to bring the gay beauty of nature into the house of worship and into the home surroundings. In this way the Jewish festivals will be enriched and the opportunities for a happy family life will be enhanced.

THOU SHALT REJOICE

Little children ask big questions. They hear the words "God" and "heaven" and "earth" and "life" long before they can understand their meaning. Only by asking can they learn, and they learn to ask early: What is God? Who is God? Where is God? But, because the answers are often given in other words which they cannot understand, their whole idea of God and the entire concept of religion is a strange and puzzling thing. It is shrouded with meanings beyond the grasp of a four-year-old. This combination of mystery and solemnity stamp indelibly on the child's mind the fact that God and religion are serious, solemn, to be spoken of with a grave manner and in big words.

So to a child religion grows to be awesome. He may make fun of the man on the corner when a snowball topples his hat. He may make fun of school because in school we laugh and play and sing. But religion! He would not make fun of religion. And so we grow up being a little afraid of it. And it is not until we are old enough to think for ourselves that we know that religion is not all sad and solemn, that religion too can be enjoyed with a spirit of light-heartedness. Indeed our wise old Rabbis said that the way to serve God is by obeying His commandments *with joyousness*.

Nowadays we try to teach the child early that besides all the wonderful and big and solemn blessings we get from our religion, we can also get gaiety, enjoyment and happiness. We are learning to give children the pleasant, the

10. A flower arrangement under the bronze memorial plaque in the Men's Club Memorial Lounge honors the war dead; it is appropriate for any patriotic occasion. The classic bronze container holds chrysanthemums and seed pods (the tips taped to sticks in a cluster to contrast with the round forms of the chrysanthemums). *Courtesy of Rodef Shalom Temple, Pittsburgh, Pa. Arranged by Mrs. J. Arthur Stein.*

charming, the joyful background which was always present in our religious tradition.

The festivals lend themselves magnificently to this joy-giving effort. The holidays are almost all happy occasions. Even where the message is a solemn one of world destiny, even where it calls for moral self-judgment, the surroundings of the festivals can be made for the child one of pleasure and enjoyment so that he grows up loving *Purim* because we laugh so heartily on *Purim*, and he waits eagerly for

11. For a formal pulpit, dual standards are strategically placed to draw the eye to the classic columns flanking the Ark. This design, using all white flowers, would create a striking setting for the High Holy Days. *Courtesy, Rodef Shalom Temple, Pittsburgh, Pa. Arranged by Mrs. James A. Frank, assisted by Mrs. Richard J. Aronson.*

Chanuko because we get such lovely presents on *Chanuko*, and he waits impatiently for *Pesach* because the whole story of the Passover is really a story for the children and is celebrated with the whole family gathered in a joyous mood.

The center of each festival is by natural selection the home. We go to the temple or synagogue for the religious services which commemorate each of the holidays, but those services are made meaningful for the child—and the adult— if the home has properly prepared him for it. If there is no excitement over the *Seder* but on Passover that meal is just like any other meal in the year, if all we say to the child is: "Come, we will go to temple or to synagogue and learn that the Israelites once were slaves in Egypt and Moses freed them from bondage," the child remembers only the saddening words "slaves" and "bondage." And he is afraid and he does not like Passover. And we have cheated ourselves, too, of the surge of feeling which comes with the celebration of the springtime festival of Passover.

But, instead, we begin talking about *Pesach* weeks before it approaches. We remind everybody what fun it is going to be to eat matzos again. We talk about whom we shall invite to the *Seder*. Since it is a holiday, we are going to make it as festive as possible and what is more festive than having company? We will wear our nicest clothes and use the best silver and the fragile china that mother brings out only for company.

We will remember to order enough wine so that everyone will have four cups of wine during the *Seder,* even the littlest child (little cups, of course). We want to start practising how to say the word *charoses* so that no one will laugh at us when we ask the Four Questions. Who will ask the Four Questions? The youngest child of the family, of course. And then father is going to hide the piece of the middle matzo, the fragment called the *Afikomen.* Who is going to find the hidden matzos and who is going to get the prize for finding it?

By the time Passover actually comes the child is more eager for the holiday than any of the adults. And then at the *Seder* we read the story to him, and he hears it again at services. We tell him that the children of Israel once were slaves but that Moses redeemed them and they were free to go forth and bring the message of God to the world. Thus the child learns happily the lesson of God's protectiveness.

FAMILY MEMORIES

Some of our loveliest memories go back to certain occasions in our family. Many of these memories find us back together around the dining table. Whether it is a special dish which mother makes for that particular festival, whether it is the sight of a flower we remember, or maybe even just the sudden appearance of the Haggadahs on the table — any one of these things can evoke in our memories those happy times when we were young and had no responsibilities, and all the world was "holiday time."

It would be sufficient, of course, to have a fine *Seder* without special table arrangements. One could still use the nice china and the freshly polished silver and arrange for the food to be different from every-day food. But so much more fun is it for the child perhaps even to participate, or to know that mother is making so many extra preparations. It becomes that much more important. He may eat ice-cream and cake on Sunday with a good Sunday dinner, but ice-cream and cake at his birthday party assume an importance they never can have at any ordinary meal. When he comes to a holiday table and finds that mother has gone to so much extra trouble to make this an unusual meal, a special occasion, then of course it is an unusual meal and a special occasion, one he will long remember.

To the child the holiday becomes a special day, a special occasion, and all the big words and solemn ideas he files away in his little mind to take out and examine again when he is old enough to understand them without being frightened by words like "awesome" and "sin" and "forgiveness."

Of course, these extra bits of trouble we may go to for the children, we also take for ourselves. Sometimes we may even use the excuse that we do these things for the children, when actually we are trying to recapture our own youthful memories. That is as good a reason for going to extra fuss at the holidays as the pedagogic one we use for the sake of the children.

We do not even have to have that reason. We do not need any more excuse than liking to set a lovely holiday table. No justification ever needs to be offered for doing anything that makes life more attractive since most of our days we spend trying to make life more beautiful. That is why people write poetry and sing songs and raise flowers. Yet in making life more gracious we make our service to God more meaningful. And so we take all the beauty we can find, the poetry and the music and the flowers, and we enhance and sanctify each festival with all of the splendor we can achieve.

In thus beautifying the festivals, it is not necessary to go to great trouble at all times for each holiday, for each meal, nor even to great expense. Sometimes the arrangement one uses may be quite simple. If there is to be company, then it may be more elaborate. We present not only the elaborate company arrangements, but also the simple arrangements made just for the family.

THE UNITY OF THE JEWISH YEAR

Some people do take a great deal of pains over one particular holiday. They will always see to it that *Chanuko,* for example, is one of the happiest occasions of the year in their home. Or it may be only Passover they take extra trouble about. But one holiday is as important as another.

There is a unity in the whole of the Jewish year that in itself achieves a cumulative significance. By making each holiday as important as we can, we make that unity compact. We do not wait in a vacuum for twelve long months for *Chanuko* to come around again. We go on to *Purim* and *Pesach* and then to *Shabuoth* and *Rosh Hashonah,* and so on, and when we have passed *Succoth,* we join the circle again with *Chanuko.* That very unity can develop profound meaning for us. We can combine the dignity and the splendors of our faith with beauty and the work of our hands and make a splendid procession of the passing year.

To teach our children the wonders of their faith, to remind ourselves of its significance, to transform our world into as glorious a garden as our hands can make possible, we add these floral arrangements and table-setting displays and home decorations for our festivals, and hope they will bring delight to the eye and joy to the heart and solace to the soul.

CHAPTER TWO

The Sabbath

THE COVENANT

IT MAY SEEM STRANGE that we begin with the Sabbath, rather than with the New Year, *Rosh Hashonah,* which opens the "Days of Awe" and begins the cycle of the Jewish religious year. We begin with the Sabbath because it is actually the holiest of all the sacred days. Every other festival was based upon the remembrance of some special event or blessing: the deliverance from Egypt, the giving of the Law, the repentance of sin. But the Sabbath is the sign of the basic covenant between Israel and God. "I gave them My Sabbath, to be a sign between Me and them, that they might know that I am the Lord that sanctify them." Once in every seven days we remember to think of God the Creator and to be aware of our covenant to be His co-workers.

Early in the Bible we are commanded: "Remember the Sabbath day to keep it holy." The Book of Jubilees describes the Sabbath as given to Jacob and his seed so that they might remain "the blessed and holy ones of the first testimony and law." And Philo said that this day was intended for God. God had devoted the seventh day for His own divine happiness, but He shares that celestial joy with man, giving him the Sabbath to be devoted to rest for the body, to bring peace to the mind, and solace to the soul.

12. The Sabbath table in all its elegance sets the day apart as the holiest one of the week. Wine and the *Kiddush* cup, the candles and the *challah* under the embroidered linen cover, comprise the Friday evening symbols with the flowers in the Steuben bowl fulfilling the statement of J. Gregory Conway: "rubrum lilies need no emphasis to reveal their beauty." *Arranged by Mrs. James A. Eckstein, Pittsburgh, Pa.*

THE FIRST SABBATH

Legend tells us that the first observance of the Sabbath took place on the very day it was created. At the end of the sixth day of creation, God ceased working. He called to Him the Angel of the Sabbath and commanded him to proclaim to all creation that henceforth the seventh day was to be the Sabbath day, a holy day. The Angel of the Sabbath delivered this commandment to all His creation, to the angels and the sea, the mountains and the rocks, to man and the beasts of the earth. Then he winged his way back to the throne of God.

"O Lord," said he, "I have given Your command to all Your creatures in all the world and have bid them come to the Sabbath and praise Ye."

Drawing 1. Basic step for arrangement in Plate 13 below.

13. In the summer, a triangular arrangement of garden flowers, yellow roses and white delphiniums, placed in a white bowl on an end table, bids welcome to Sabbath guests. *Arranged by Mrs. James A. Eckstein, Pittsburgh, Pa.*

Thus it was that on the morrow, the very first Sabbath, everything in the universe rested from its labors. God rested from creating. The fires stopped burning. The bees refrained from gathering their honey. The winds were gentle, all the earth rested, and the sea was quiet. Everyone sang in harmony and in unity their hymn of praise to God. And thus they celebrated the first Sabbath.

THE STRUGGLE FOR A DAY OF REST

This charming story of how God ordained and proclaimed the Sabbath is, of course, a legend. Between its ordaining and its actual acceptance by man there was a long and hard-fought battle.

In our day, so usual, so customary a thing is the resting one day a week that most people believe that it was always so. Actually, it was a struggle to establish it. Solomon B. Freehof in his book, *The Small Sanctuary,* expresses it:

> The Sabbath was unique as an institution and was recognized as unique as soon as the Jews came in contact with the Greco-Roman world. We who are so accustomed to the idea of resting one day a week almost feel that it is inherent in nature and can hardly realize what life would be like if the days went on in unbroken succession with no regular grouping or division for variety and rest. But thus, indeed, it was in the western world before the Jewish influence, directly through Judaism and later through the daughter-religion Christianity [that the idea of a day of rest] made itself felt. In Rome those who owned slaves never worked, and those who were slaves never rested. The idea that all human beings ... have the right and the duty to rest one day in seven was a new and startling idea. ... Roman writers said many bitter things about it. ... They sneered at the growing demand of slaves for a rest every seventh day; but the Sabbath could not be laughed away. Once it was made known to the world it was bound to be accepted, for it was based upon the right of man as a child of God Who rested on the Seventh day of the Creation of the world. The humane institution of the Sabbath thus left its permanent mark upon civilization.

14. A brass Sabbath lamp holds fresh and dried materials: summer squash, fake jewels, gold sprayed wheat burrs, small seed pods, milkweed pods and ivy. The center of interest is created by "flowers" made of summer squash transformed into an elegant accessory by spraying the edges gold (a cardboard disc pinned to center keeps it to natural color) and then fastening fake jewels around core. A heavy wire, run through the back of the squash, is twisted into the arrangement. Lightly gilded ivy, well-sprayed pods, and flowers made of split peach seeds, complete the composition for a gala occasion. *Arranged by Mrs. J. Arthur Stein, Pittsburgh, Pa.*

15. In the fall, an arrangement of fruits, flowers and Sabbath candles decorates the table. Sprays of leaves and glistening fruit in the motif of the Star of David form the base, with one large dahlia nesting among the candles. The arrangement is tall enough so that flickering candles do not shine in the eyes of seated guests. *Arranged by Rae L. Goldson, Woodmere, N. Y.*

16. "Remember the Sabbath day to keep it holy." This festive dinner table inaugurates the Sabbath in a reverent mood. Heirloom silver holds pussywillows, peach blossoms, pink sweet peas and pink ranunculi—all heralding springtime. *Arranged by Mrs. Richard Dinner, San Francisco, Calif.*

SABBATH PEACE

Had the Sabbath remained merely a day of rest it could easily have become a day of gloom and misery. After all, work was prohibited, the lighting of fire was forbidden; what then was there to do? So the Talmud made careful provision for the day to become happy and merry. It recommended the finest of foods and the finest of clothing, no fasting, no sorrowing, instead, the singing of songs, the worship of God with joy. Indeed, even mourning for a dear one must be interrupted for the Sabbath.

The Sabbath is a day for the rebuilding of the spirit. Again we quote from *The Small Sanctuary*, "It is a day of radiant spiritual peace. Sabbath rest is not idleness, it is the serenity of the soul. It is a God-given gift."

Judaism had for a short time in its history a period of

kings and monarchs but they departed so long ago we read of them only in the Bible. But Judaism has a Queen, and the Queen is the Sabbath. Sometimes the Sabbath is called the Bride and always it is known as the Queen. And to the Queen once a week we pay homage.

All Jewish festivals begin at sundown on the evening before. On the Sabbath, to be certain that the holy shall not be profaned, one hour of Friday is added beforehand. This is called "adding from the profane to the holy." On the principle that we can never be holy enough, there is no harm in observing the Sabbath for one hour more than is necessary.

Late on Friday afternoon we prepare to greet the Queen, the Sabbath. The Sabbath meal is, traditionally, the finest meal of the week. To it we bring our best china, our best food and our best selves. Whenever people are happy, they want to share their happiness. And they invite their friends. So most frequently guests are invited to the Sabbath meal.

THE FRIDAY EVE RITUAL

The table is set with a festive cloth. The bread is placed on the table covered with a white napkin, or an especially embroidered cover, until it is time to pronounce the blessings. The traditional bread, the *challah,* is usually long and braided. German women in the early Middle Ages baked braided loaves of bread in honor of the goddess of vegetation, Berchta. The Jewish women in Germany baked these loaves for the Sabbath, calling them by the same name, *berches.* However, some interpret the name as being connected with the word *broches,* meaning blessing, which is recited over the bread.

Since then this meal is to be different from all other meals of the week, there is an added charm in serving a bread one does not eat all during the week, a bread that is baked specially for it.

In front of the father's place is set the *Kiddush* cup for the wine ceremony. This cup may be fashioned of gold or silver or crystal. Candles may be placed in silver or crystal candlesticks. Many people, out of sentiment, remembering the Sabbath tables of their grandmothers or their mothers prefer to use brass candlesticks. In the Rhineland a hanging star-shaped oil-lamp was used. The Sabbath light has been spoken of as "the Sabbath lamp," but there is no requirement that it be a lamp or candles, nor is there a limitation to the number of candles we burn. Some of our ancestors lighted a candle for each child born into her family and thus may have used seven or eight candlesticks, or three or two. But there must be a minimum of two lights since the Ten Commandments, which include the commandment to observe the Sabbath, is found in two places in the Torah, in Exodus and in Deuteronomy. In one place the commandment begins: "Remember the Sabbath Day," and in the other the commandment begins: "Observe the Sabbath day." These two different verses are given as the reason for using at least two lights.

The candlesticks, whether brass or silver or crystal, should be polished brightly and fitted with thick white candles. The Sabbath candles may not be extinguished when the meal is finished but must burn out themselves. Nor may they be used for a practical purpose, to light other lights, or to read by.

The mother lights the candles. It is her duty and it is a duty which becomes a privilege. In the absence of the mother from the home, the father may light the candles. At sundown, when the family has gathered around the table and the Friday evening service is about to begin, the mother

17. A flower arrangement in the oriental manner decorates the home for the Sabbath. Flowers could be changed according to seasonal availability. *Arranged by Temple Shalom Garden Club, West Newton, Mass.*

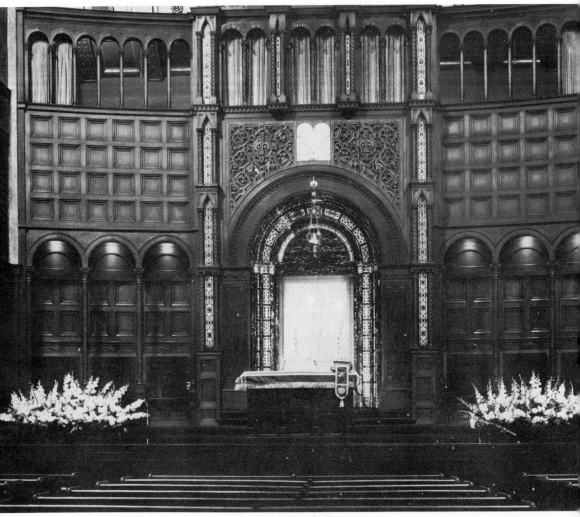

18. Twin arrangements of yellow chrysanthemums and orange gladioli, in metal containers faced with black marble to match the altar, echo the arches of the pulpit on a Sabbath evening. *Courtesy, Wilshire Boulevard Temple, Los Angeles, Calif.*

lights the Sabbath candles and recites a prayer, followed by the blessing. The following is a modernized form of the traditional ritual:

Thou art our Light, O Lord, and our Salvation. In Thy name we kindle these Sabbath lights. May they bring into our household the beauty of truth and the radiance of love's understanding. On this Sabbath eve and at all times, 'Let there be light.'

Boruch atto adonoi elohenu melech ho'olom asher kid'shonu b'mitzvosov vetzivohnu l'hadlik nayr shel shabbos.

Praised be Thou, Lord our God, King of the Universe, Who has sanctified us with Thy commandments and commanded us to kindle the light of the Sabbath.

The father raises the *Kiddush* cup of wine and recites a prayer, then the blessing over the wine:

Wine is the symbol of joy. On Sabbaths and festivals in the ancient temple and in all the homes of Israel, our fathers lifted up the cup of happiness and proclaimed the name of the Lord. At His command they rose above their sorrows and honored the holy day with heartfelt joy. On this day we ask of Thee, O God, to shield us from sickness and sorrow. Strengthen us with Thy help and gladden us with Thy blessing. In our hearts and in our homes let this be a Sabbath of joy.

Boruch atto adonoi elohenu melech ho'olom boray p'ree hagofen.

Praised be Thou, Lord our God, King of the Universe, Who hast created the fruit of the vine.

After each one has taken a sip of the wine, it is time for the child to participate in the service. The unbroken loaf of bread is placed before him and he recites the following prayer and blessing over the bread.

Bread is the staff of life. The wheat, the corn, and all the food which grows from the earth are the sign of God's blessing and the fruit of human work. For the bounty of nature's harvest, which rewards the work of man, we utter our thanks to the Father Eternal.

Boruch atto adonoi elohenu melech ho'olom hamotzi lechemin ho'oretz.

Praised be Thou, Lord our God, King of the Universe, Who bringest forth food from the earth.

The father slices the bread and distributes a piece to each person at the table and in the household. (These

19. After the dedication service of its new synagogue building, the congregation participated in a reception held in the beige marble-walled foyer. A gold net cloth and golden candelabra enhanced the three-tiered arrangement with its sprays of laurel, privet, gladioli, and chrysanthemums anchored in a gilded pineapple jewelled with corsage pins. The graduated lower tiers, using the same materials, were effectively sprayed with gold for over-all brilliance. *Courtesy of Tree of Life Synagogue, Pittsburgh, Pa. Arranged by Mrs. Benjamin M. Clasky.*

prayers have been taken from *The Friday Evening Home Service* by Solomon B. Freehof.)

Thus the Sabbath Queen has been ushered into the home, to reign for twenty-four hours. After dinner the family goes to the temple or the synagogue to participate in the late Friday evening services. And also, on the following morning, the family attends services in the temple or in the synagogue.

HAVDALAH — THE "SEPARATION" OF THE SABBATH

The Sabbath day has been spent at services and in the refreshment of the spirit. And then the day begins to come to a close and, as the sun sets, there occurs in more traditional homes, and now also in the Reform Youth Camps, the *Havdalah* service.

The Hebrew word *Havdalah* means separation or distinction. It is the home ceremony which divides the sacred—the Sabbath—from the commonplace or mundane week and distinguishes as well between the greater sacredness of the Sabbath and the lesser sacredness of the festivals.

The Bible, in Deuteronomy (28:6), states: "Blessed shalt thou be when thou comest in, and blessed shalt thou be when thou goest out." Hence the *Havdalah* service at the close of the Sabbath balances the Friday evening ritual at the introduction of the Sabbath.

20. For a Friday evening reception, the *Oneg Shabbat* following services, an off-white linen cloth and napkins embroidered with numerous Jewish motifs are a perfect setting for the antique seven-branched Sabbath *Menorah* with flowers placed in some of the cups and white candles glowing in the others. Table balance is achieved by the brass samovar and grouped cups and saucers brightly decorated with ivy. A triangle of white chrysanthemums, sprays of green and white dracaena, and pendant bunches of white grapes complete the arrangement. A treasured Bible is an accessory. *Arranged by Mrs. Albert I. Raizman, Pittsburgh, Pa.*

21. *Havdalah.* The graceful floral composition of white Fuji chrysanthemums with Scotch broom forming a Hogarth line is placed in an antique silver goblet resting on a blue-bordered plate. The blue and white twisted *Havdalah* candle and the spice box, or *Besamim*, are specific items used in the service. The plate is useful as well as decorative. *Arranged by Mrs. Louis J. Hoechstetter, Pittsburgh, Pa.*

There are four symbols of the *Havdalah* service: the twisted candle, the spice box, the special dish, and the wine cup. After the blessing has been made over the wine, the wine is tasted and what is left in the cup is poured into the special dish. After the blessing for light has been pronounced and the candle has been lighted, it is then extinguished in the wine in the special dish.

The twisted candle is usually made up of two or more colors. Four very slender tapers are wound together. This candle is not meant to be placed in a holder, but is held in the hand during the brief part of the service when it is used. Many people have questioned its composition of more than one taper. It has been suggested that the reason for the multiple candle is the fact that the *Havdalah* light blessing itself uses the plural, "the lights of the fire."

The best known symbol of the *Havdalah* service is the spice or *Besamim* box (*Besamim* means spice). Some of the most beautiful ceremonial objects to be found amongst all the symbols of Jewish ritual are the spice boxes of various shapes. Generally the *Besamim* boxes are in the shape of a tower, sometimes in the shape of a stag, based upon the verse in Song of Songs, "My beloved is like the stag on the mountains of spices." Some are shaped like silver fish. A great deal of artistry has gone into the creation of these spice boxes. In them are kept sweet spices which we smell to strengthen us for the week of work because the "extra soul" granted on the Sabbath departs and leaves us faint; therefore may we be strengthened by the sweet spices.

THE HAVDALAH SERVICE

The head of the household conducts the *Havdalah* service. He takes the cup of wine in his right hand and pronounces the blessing:

Behold, God is my salvation; I will trust, and will not be afraid:

22. The vogue for using "permanent" flowers, leaves and fruit is practical when fresh flowers are not available. This contemporary grouping of strelitzias, leaves and a cluster of small citrus fruits brightens the winter Sabbath eve. *Arranged by Mrs. Samuel Roth, Pittsburgh, Pa.*

for Jah the Lord is my strength and song, and he is become my salvation. Therefore with joy shall ye draw water out of the wells of salvation. Salvation belongeth unto the Lord: thy blessing be upon thy people. (Selah.) The Lord of hosts is with us, the God of Jacob is our refuge. (Selah.) The Jews had light and joy and gladness and honour. So be it with us. I will lift the cup of salvation, and call upon the name of the Lord.

Boruch atto adonoi elohenu melech ho'olom boray pri hagofen.

Blessed art thou, O Lord our God, King of the Universe, who createst the fruit of the vine.

The spice box is taken into the hand, and the following blessing is recited:

Boruch atto adonoi elohenu melech ho'olom boray minay v'sawmim.

Blessed art thou, O Lord our God, King of the Universe, who createst divers kinds of spices.

The hands are spread towards the light, and the following is said:

Boruch atto adononi elohenu melech ho'olom boray m'oray hawesh.

Blessed art thou, O Lord our God, King of the Universe, who createst the light of the fire.

The cup is again taken in the right hand, and the following verse is given:

Boruch atto adonoi elohenu melech ho'olom hamavdil bayn kodesh l'chol bayn or l'choshech.

Blessed art thou, O Lord our God, King of the Universe, who makest a distinction between holy and profane, between light and darkness, between Israel and other nations.

The Sabbath has ended and we wish each other a good week to come. (Some of these blessings are from the *Singer Authorized Daily Prayerbook.*)

CHAPTER THREE

Rosh Hashonah, the New Year

THE DAYS OF AWE

THE JEWISH RELIGIOUS YEAR begins with solemn days. The later holidays and the pilgrim festivals are times of rejoicing but the beginning of a new year comes with a solemn spiritual mood and serious self-searching.

The New Year, *Rosh Hashonah,* and the Day of Atonement, *Yom Kippur,* the High Holy Days, are called the Awesome Days *(Yamim Noroim).* They occur during the first ten days of the month of *Tishri,* in the English calendar anywhere from the middle of September to early October (depending on the relation between the lunar and the solar calendars). Between the New Year and the Day of Atonement are the ten Days of Penitence.

This whole period is devoted to deep and sincere self-judgment in the presence of the Judge of the world. During this time we seek out our faults and our failings. We admit our mistakes and confess our sins. We ask for pardon and we promise to try to become "a kingdom of priests and a holy people."

23. The *Shofar,* interpreted in crystal, enhances the elegance of the crystal and china on the table. Red ginger picks up the wheat pattern in the cloth and napkins, and a madonna lily is used for contrast. Candles, wine, *challah,* honey and apple complete the holiday symbols. *Arranged by Mrs. Marcia Meyers, Pittsburgh, Pa.*

HAPPY NEW YEAR! — L'SHONO TOVO!

The summer is over. Everyone has returned from vacations. School has started for the youngsters. Everyone is ready to begin another season and we start it off by wishing each other a good and a happy new year.

The origins of *Rosh Hashonah* are found only partially in the Bible. This holiday is much more the product of the synagogue through the Prayerbook. In the Bible in Leviticus there is the command: "In the seventh month, in the first day of the month, shall be a solemn rest unto you, a memorial proclaimed with the blast of horns, a holy convocation." This command, and references in Numbers and Nehemiah, combining the ideas of a day of rest, a sounding of trumpets and a holy convocation, became the foundation on which the entire New Year service was built.

The authors of the Prayerbook wove these ideas and the hope of universal brotherhood into one of the greatest spiritual influences in the life of Israel. They brought the highest vision of the prophets, that of the universalistic ideal of human brotherhood, into the Prayerbook and thus into daily life. All mankind has One Father. Some day we will realize our common brotherhood. Some day we will acknowledge that fraternity by beating our swords into ploughshares and when that day comes we shall have formed one united family and we shall then worship One God.

THE SHOFAR

The shofar is a ram's horn which we blow on the High Holy Days. Each year it calls us to come and stand before God's judgment throne. We are summoned to come individually and be judged because, until we know our own sins, until we learn to wipe out our own mistakes, we cannot forgive others, we cannot form a united family. On this day all the world, newborn, stands before God's judgment throne. *Rosh Hashonah* is a day of accounting, year after year, rather than a long-range concept of a far distant day of *world* judgment. The vision of the ennobled and united humanity will remain only a vision unless the world is built upon the foundations of a purified human character, as the Prayerbook says: "To rebuild the world under the dominion of the Almighty."

Thus the New Year is a festival on which the spiritual life of the *individual* is emphasized. On this holiday we say, "May *you* have a happy new year." The Hebrew word for

24. Autumn is ushered in with this stylized design of dried material placed in an antique vase on an oriental scroll base. The palmetto leaves, sprayed gold, suggest the rhythm; the fruits and flowers form the center of interest. Nuts wired into grape-like bunches, black and green grapes, small pineapples, love apples, ferns, green cycas leaves and a lotus blossom complete the composition. *Arranged by Mrs. Harry M. Aronson, Pittsburgh, Pa.*

"happy" means mainly "good." We wish our friends a year of goodness because only out of goodness can happiness come.

THE BOOK OF LIFE

On this "day of awe," we are especially concerned with thoughts of continuing life. We think of "The Book of Life" in which we hope our name has been inscribed for this new year. To that end the day is awesome for us because we pray for life, the gift from God. We are solemn as we hope for this unique and precious gift for yet another year. But once we have hoped and prayed, since now it is in God's Hands, we turn aside in a happy mood to savor the holiday for the joy it brings.

25. The circle, having neither beginning nor ending, symbolizes eternity, so the circular table for a *Rosh Hashonah* Eve dinner is appropriate. It is adorned with pink dahlias and laurel. The tall white candles lend distinction to the design and are an essential symbol for the festive table, along with the round *challah* concealed by the hand-embroidered cover, the wine, the apple and the honey. The silver goblet at the host's place is from Israel. *Arranged by Mrs. Robert I. Hiller, Pittsburgh, Pa.*

26. This festive arrangement in tints and tones of gold and yellows is bursting with good wishes for the *Rosh Hashonah* congregants. Chrysanthemums (yellow Fuji and spider, and rust-colored pompons), yellow gladioli, gilded sprays of Scotch broom and rhododendron and lemon leaves, are the "sunny" plant materials. The white holiday pulpit desk cover, the silver Torah crowns, and the Star of David (*Mogen Dovid*) embroidered on the Bible marker attract the attention of the holiday worshippers. *Courtesy of Temple Israel, New Rochelle, N.Y. Arranged by Mrs. David Kirschenbaum, Harrison, N.Y.*

We put our thoughts to earthly gifts. *Rosh Hashonah* is one of the happy, gift-giving holidays. To have prayed for life brings a feeling of comfort; to look forward with zest to the mysteries of a new year brings a feeling of adventure; and in our joy and enthusiasm we want to share. We buy presents for the children and receive them from our friends.

We beautify our homes and decorate them with greens and blossoms. In the fourteenth century it was the custom to weave baskets of palm leaves, fill them with soil and plant beans or peas fifteen or twenty days before *Rosh Hashonah*. Nowadays we use plants and flowers to grace the home, to lighten our spirits, and to remind ourselves of the wonder of God's generous and ever-renewing bounty.

27. To greet the New Year, members of the congregation are received in the Solomon B. Freehof Hall where a buffet table holds light refreshments, as well as a modern arrangement of yellow Fuji chrysanthemums, Scotch broom, begonia leaves and *Pieris japonica* foliage on a silver base. Sparkling bright hand-wrought silver candelabra and tall white candles denote the pristine newness of the year. *Courtesy, Rodef Shalom Temple, Pittsburgh, Pa. Arranged by Mrs. Bernard Mallinger and Mrs. Herbert R. Rosenthal.*

Weeks before the holiday starts we surround ourselves with the glow of the new and the unknown. We do not wait until just the day before *Rosh Hashonah* to begin thinking about the holiday, but we start long in advance. We send cards to our friends, and with each card or letter or gift, we say, "Happy New Year," and our own spirits are lifted day by day.

A SWEET YEAR

We start the year off with a happy holiday meal which precedes the services at the temple or synagogue. Again we spice the air with the cooking of the choicest foods. Out come our best silver and china. The table is set again with candlesticks but we do not say the blessings. On *Rosh Hashonah* candles may be lighted but no blessing is recited. There is *Kiddush,* however, and the father blesses the wine and the special *round* loaf of bread.

For the New Year the *challah* is made round, symbolizing the hope that the new year which is coming may be smooth, without difficulties, and round, without cessation. Near the father's place is set a dish in which there is honey and another dish of quartered apples. After the candles have been lighted, and the wine and the bread have been blessed, the father dips a piece of the apple into the honey for each member of the household and recites the following blessing:

Y'hi rotzon she'techadesh lonu shono tovo u mesukah.

May it be Thy will, O Lord, to renew for us a good and a sweet year.

After dinner the family goes to the services at temple or synagogue at which they pray the holiday ritual, hear special holiday music and an appropriate holiday sermon. After the benediction has been pronounced by the Rabbi, each person turns and wishes his family and his friends a very happy new year.

CHAPTER FOUR

Yom Kippur, the Day of Atonement

THE SABBATH OF SABBATHS

Yom Kippur, the Day of Atonement, is the most solemn occasion in the Jewish year, the true "day of awe." It is called "The Sabbath of Solemn Rest," or "The Sabbath of Sabbaths."

It is more closely connected with the Bible than *Rosh Hashonah*. In Leviticus, after prohibiting work and calling for a holy convocation, it is commanded: "Ye shall afflict your souls . . . for it is a Day of Atonement for you before the Lord your God." During the *Yom Kippur* services the reading in Leviticus describes the ritual for this day. The prophetic portion in Isaiah details the ethical implications of sincere fasting: "Is this the fast I have chosen?" The theme of the Book of Jonah, which is read in the afternoon service, deals with the repentance of the pagan city of Nineveh, fitting the universalistic note of the high holiday season. All who come to God in sincere repentance will be received in forgiveness.

On this day we make the most earnest effort of the year to search our own souls and to admit our sins for which we seek forgiveness. Worshipping in the synagogue, each person tries to achieve atonement by his own sincerity of

28. A *Kol Nidrei* Dinner Table. On the linen damask cloth are fine china, silver and crystal, with place cards made in the shape of a dove. (In the Bible, Israel is referred to as a dove, and on *Yom Kippur* the Book of Jonah is read. Jonah means dove; thus the dove is suggested as the motif for the place cards.) Other essential symbols for this holiday meal are the round *challah* (loaf of bread), the wine, and the candles. A silver *Kiddush* cup is set for the male guest as well as for the host. The large flat white bowl resting on a bamboo base contains white snapdragons and pompons in pieces of cured cherry wood. *Arranged by Mrs. Frederick C. Schwartz, Pittsburgh, Pa.*

thought and intention. These prayers for self-purification have been the spiritual practice of Israel down through the centuries. Included in them are those naturally which touch on our dealings with our fellow man. Before the Day of Atonement can effect cleansing of the heart, a man must first undo whatever ill he has done to any one else; as the Mishnah says, sins that are between man and God, the Day of Atonement atones, but sins that are between man and his fellow-man, the Day of Atonement does not atone until he appeases his fellow-man.

On so solemn an occasion it would be impossible to achieve a spirit of gaiety, nor is it even permitted. This day is meant to be spent in fasting and confession and atonement.

THE CESSATION MEAL

The evening service at the temple or synagogue is called *Kol Nidrei,* the time for the releasing of *ritual* vows (*Kol Nidrei* means all vows). But before the *Kol Nidrei* service, the meal which is a preparation for the fast is considered a festival meal. It is called *Seudah Hammafseketh,* the cessation meal. There is no prohibition to its being a somewhat festive occasion.

The table may be as carefully planned as for any other festival. Indeed there must be candles because on *Yom Kippur* the candles are kindled and the following blessing recited:

> *Boruch atto adonoi elohenu melech ho'olom asher kid' shonu b'mitzvosov vetzivohnu l'hadlik nayr shel yom kippurim.*
>
> Praised be Thou O Lord our God, King of the Universe, Who has sanctified us by His commandments and has commanded us to kindle the lights of Yom Kippur.

Flowers may grace the table. There is the blessing recited over bread.

It is on the next day, on the Day of Atonement itself, on which we are required not to feast and not to rejoice, but to spend the day in meditation and in prayer and in fasting. But on *Kol Nidrei* Eve the meal is a Sabbath meal, for it is a Sabbath of Sabbaths.

29. This dried arrangement is the harvest of summer plant growth. Bayberry branches and milkweed, with yarrow for the center of interest—a stunning combination of shiny green, mustard brown and white—are woven into a pleasing triangular pattern. When the milkweed pods were opened and the outer casing, seeds and fluff removed, the effect was one of birds in flight. Such an arrangement may be used in the home for any autumn festival. *Arranged by Mrs. Jerome E. Markstein, Pittsburgh, Pa.*

31. The ram's horn and the *lulav* encircling the Hebrew scroll, King Protea flowers (which come from near the Holy Land) and E-Koa pods on moss placed on a wooden base, make an unusual home decoration for the Day of Atonement and *Succoth*. *Arranged by Mrs. William H. Loveman, Shaker Heights, Ohio.*

30. Dinner before the *Kol Nidrei* service is a festive occasion. Wine, *challah*, and candles are essential symbols. Here, the flowers are placed in the center of a five-branched Victorian candelabrum. Pale pink gladioli, chrysanthemums and carnations blend with the deep pink satin damask cloth and the gold encrusted crystal and china. Because of the height of the candelabrum, the floral arrangement (placed in Oasis) rises above the heads of the guests. *Arranged by Mrs. Harry D. Rice, Pittsburgh, Pa.*

CHAPTER FIVE

Succoth, the Feast of the Harvest

THE PILGRIM FESTIVALS

THE THREE MOST ancient festivals, *Succoth, Shabuoth* and Passover, are the agricultural festivals. They are the outcome of a long and complex historical development.

Originally they were primitive pastoral holidays, celebrated when the people of Israel were shepherds. Later, when they became a settled farmer people in Palestine, came the evidences of agricultural development. And still later was added the historical implication to each occasion. Now, in our time, all the origins are completely interwoven and the themes form a unit.

These three holidays are called the Pilgrim Festivals because the Bible clearly commanded each Israelite to appear three times a year, at *Succoth, Shabuoth* and Passover, at the temple in Jerusalem. The people travelled many, many miles on their pilgrimages to Jerusalem and the temple and the celebration. Each occasion came at a significant time in the agricultural year. Passover occurred at the close of winter and the beginning of spring when barley, the earliest grain, ripened. *Shabuoth* marked the end of the grain harvest and the beginning of the fruit harvest. *Succoth* represented the end of all harvests.

32. Dominant and symbolic in the composition are the dried palm branch (a *lulav*) and the citrus fruit (lemons). The glycerined broom in the background strengthens the tall vertical "line of aspiration" established by the palm. Other materials include bleached okra pods, glycerined leaves and lotus pods. The container is a narrow-necked Israeli pottery ewer in black, white and brown, set on a small, heavy base of polished myrtle wood, also from Israel. Since *Succoth* is a week-long festival, this arrangement would easily last through the holiday. *Arranged by Mrs. Milton Lang, Shaker Heights, Ohio.*

The greatest emphasis now in our day, however, is to be found in the historical significance of each holiday. All three are described as "a memorial of the going out from Egypt." Passover deals with the deliverance from Egypt itself, the actual Exodus: "The time of our freedom." *Shabuoth* deals with the giving of the Law on Mount Sinai: "The time of the giving of our law." *Succoth* was concerned with the dwelling in booths in the desert: "The time of our rejoicing."

The spirit of the three festivals as expressed in the synagogue service is a blending of the two traditional moods: the year of nature as manifested in the harvest and the events of Israel's history. The Bible and the synagogue take the universal mood of hilarity at harvest time and convert it into a divinely ordained duty to rejoice with full heart and with generous sharing of God's gifts.

SUCCOTH

After the Days of Awe have passed, the religious year con-

33. An effective pulpit decoration for the harvest festival. Elsewhere in the temple a *Succah* has been erected to portray the "dwelling in booths." The actual harvest emphasis finds its expression in this altar arrangement for the services during *Succoth*. Note the pyramidal contour, the "reaching up" in gratitude for a plentiful harvest. *Courtesy, Temple Emanu-El, Montreal, Canada.*

34. A miniature *Succah* is the centerpiece for a home dinner table. The frame of brass rods is decorated with wheat and orange-red gladioli. Mesh forms the body from which are hung red and green miniature peppers and crab apples and pyracantha berries. At the base of the booth, brass cornucopias spill out their harvest of light green and purple grapes. Inside the *Succah* is a miniature table with a brass candlestick and orange candle, symbolic of the fulfillment of the commandment to dwell under the *Succah*. An emerald green, fruit-embroidered cloth, napkins outlining the cornucopias, bronze plates, bronze and horn cutlery, and green and gold glasses complete the picture. *Arranged by Mrs. Harry I. Miller, Pittsburgh, Pa.*

tinues with the agricultural festival of *Succoth*. The celebration begins on the fifteenth of *Tishri*, four days after *Yom Kippur*. It is the most joyous and festive of the holidays, in fact it is the one which is specifically described as "the time of our rejoicing."

The name *Succoth* means booths. When the people of Israel were delivered from the land of Egypt, during their long march in the desert, in the wilderness they dwelt in booths. Thus on *Succoth* we are instructed to build in the

35. The blessings of nature are richly represented in this horizontal display of assorted fruits on a *Succoth* dinner table with clusters of leaves, tall candles and a pineapple to complete an attractive picture. *Arranged by Rae L. Goldson, Woodmere, N. Y.*

open air a booth in which we shall dwell for seven days while we commemorate the life of the Israelites in the desert.

This historical reference is bound up with the agricultural reference. The harvesters of the crops in ancient Palestine would stay in the field and dwell in the booths so that the crops could be gathered in rapidly and not be spoiled by the rain, since harvesting came at the beginning of the rainy season. Thus the *Succah,* the booth, refers both to the ancient booth in the desert on the march from Egypt and to the harvesters' booths in Palestine.

Succoth occurs when the harvest has been garnered. Out of joy at having had so fruitful a season, we build the *Succah,* the booth, out in the open, with an open-latticed roof so that the sky shall not be shut out from us, so that we may dwell under the stars.

But, of course, in modern times the building of a *Succah* by an individual family has become virtually impossible. Those of our fellow Jews who are suburbanites are able, of course, to build an outdoor *Succah*. But a large proportion of the Jews in America are urban people, living in crowded cities where land becomes precious so that houses get smaller and the land around the house gets less and less until finally most people live in apartment buildings with no land on which to build a *Succah*. The building of and the living in a *Succah* were most natural when our ancestors were farmers, all of them, or most of them, and they dwelt "by their own vine and fig tree," and it was practical too for our grandfathers before city life became so complicated and so crowded.

Nowadays many communities leave the building of the *Succah* to the temple or synagogue. In our own homes we celebrate the holiday as best as we can in our special table and home decorations. Charming ideas are workable for the construction of little *Succahs* which can be placed on the table or the mantelpiece, or the coffee table. Still other ideas are practical using the miniature *Succah*.

THE SUCCOTH SYMBOLS

Any *Succah* we may build, either in our gardens if we have them, or in a miniature form for our tables, like the large *Succah* we build in the temple or synagogue, symbolizes simplicity, frailty and humility.

The *Succah* is a booth covered with green branches and decorated with fruits. Four articles especially are used for the celebration of the festival, the *etrog*, the *lulav*, the *hadassah* (the myrtle) and the *aravah* (the willow).

Etrog

The *etrog* is a citron. It is the fruit of a tree of the orange

Drawing 2. First step in making the center arrangement shown in Plate 36.

Drawing 3. Second step in making the center arrangement shown in Plate 36.

and lemon family. The Rabbis of old fancifully suggested that the *etrog* (which is also called Adam's Apple or Paradise Apple) was the forbidden fruit eaten by Adam and Eve.

A beautiful container, either of gold or silver or other metals, is always used for the *etrog*. The Jewish artistic instinct which was kept suppressed in the pictorial arts for

36. After the framework of the *Succah* was erected and covered with cornstalks and a sparsely filled roof with autumn leaves, the ladies of the sisterhood completed the decoration as a labor of love. Trellises with espaliered *Menorahs* of lemons and lemon leaves add interest to the background. The yellow chrysanthemums with eucalyptus sprays in front of the pulpit desk tie in with gold horns of plenty which pour forth their luxurious supply of fruits and vegetables. These range from purple to red to orange and on to the lighter colors. Smaller fruits hang from the cover of the *Succah* in front of the Ark with its Torahs in holiday garb. The *lulav* (myrtle, willow and palm) and the *etrog* (citron) are placed on the pulpit desk for the Rabbi to display during the services. *Courtesy, Rodef Shalom Temple, Pittsburgh, Pa. Arranged by Rodef Shalom Sisterhood.*

37. Members of the parent-teacher association decorated a *Succah* on the stage of the auditorium in the J. Leonard Levy Hall of the temple for the religious school assembly. The footlights brought into sharp relief the traditional structure placed around a temporary Ark and reading desk. The black backdrop served as an excellent foil for the colorful bounty of the harvest. *Courtesy, Rodef Shalom Temple, Pittsburgh, Pa.*

a long time because of biblical prohibition, expressed itself in the creation of wonderful metal containers, usually silver, for the *etrog*.

LULAV

The *lulav* is the shoot of a palm tree in its folded state before the leaves are spread out. It must be at least three handbreadths long and must be bound with a twig or a tendril of its own kind. During the services in the synagogue, the *lulav* is shaken in four directions, north, south, east and west, as an acknowledgment of God's sovereignty over nature. The use of the *lulav* is ordained in Leviticus (XXIII, 40):

And ye shall take you on the first day the fruit of goodly trees, branches of palm trees, and the boughs of thick trees, and willows of the brook: and ye shall rejoice before the Lord your God seven days.

HADASSAH AND ARAVAH

The *hadassah* is composed of three twigs of myrtle of the species which has its leaves in whirls of three; and the *aravah* of two willow branches. There is a triple holder of braided palm leaves which supports the *lulav* in the center, the *hadassah* to the right and the *aravah* to the left.

REJOICING IN THE HOME

Since *Succoth* is primarily a harvest festival, and therefore one which included the people as a whole, it has become more of a temple or synagogue festival than a home festival. But the home, too, may make it beautiful in various ways in table decorations and home ornamentation.

38. Indoors, the *Succah* on the lower level of the altar has a fragile beauty. Several massed arrangements of fruits, vegetables and flowers are in perfect balance. *Courtesy, Temple Emanu-El, San Francisco, Calif. Arranged by Mrs. Leonard M. Tivol.*

FESTIVAL OF INGATHERING

For the proper celebration of this festival, one must go to temple or synagogue. Even in earliest times this holiday, the Festival of Ingathering, was observed beautifully in the sanctuary. Modern Reform services are conducted on the first and the last days of the festival. During the day of the eve of *Succoth* the women in the sisterhood decorate the *Succah*. As a rule the fruits and vegetables and flowers to be used are donated by a member of the temple or synagogue in memory of a loved one or they are provided by the sisterhood.

The *Succah* is built on the altar, over the pulpit, made of four uprights with an open roof. This is covered with autumn leaves which form the lattice work for the roof, and with sheaves of wheat and corn. Hanging from the beams of the ceiling are fruits, pears and crabapples and grapes, white and red, and certain vegetables which can be tied on string, such as green and red peppers, and so forth. All around the *Succah* are placed the fruits and vegetables.

Many of the Conservative and Orthodox congregations build their *Succahs* out-of-doors.

CHILDREN'S SERVICE

Later in the afternoon of *Succoth* Eve many congregations conduct a *Succoth* service for the children, a charming, brief service, during which the symbols of the holiday are displayed and explained. In many temples the custom has arisen to make this a consecration service for the children who are entering the religious school for the first time. The children are given flowers or palm branches to carry. They march through the temple up to the pulpit and under the *Succah* where they are blessed by the Rabbi. He then explains the various *Succoth* symbols to them, weaving in a

39. A more elaborately decorated *Succah* on the altar of the same temple shows pyramidal designs of fruits and cornstalks and standards holding twin designs of cattails, tritomas and palms. The arched *Succah* with its hanging fruits is flanked by cornstalks and airy palms. The harvest picture is completed by the fruits and vegetables. The Torah is read from the desk on the upper level. *Courtesy, Temple Emanu-El, San Francisco, Calif. Arranged by Mrs. Leonard M. Tivol.*

40. This handsome *Succah,* harmonious with the background of the temple pulpit, is composed of varied autumn treasures. Here the cornucopias spill out their lushness from the uprights toward the pulpit desk, in front of which a symmetrical arrangement of large and small yellow chrysanthemums adds the final touch of color. At either end of the pulpit is an urn of rhododendron branches. *Courtesy, Rodeph Shalom Temple, Philadelphia, Pa.*

simple and brief sermonette. Some congregations at the close of this service give all the children a large red apple as the symbol of the harvest festival.

REJOICE IN THE LAW

The *Succoth* services for adults are held the following day, with special music which regular worshippers wait for from one festival to another. The sermon, of course, is a message bearing on the holiday. At the conclusion of the services the Rabbi invites the congregation to come up to the pulpit and walk under the *Succah* to greet him. Each worshipper comes and "dwells" in the *Succah* for a minute or so, greeting the

Rabbi, examining the *Succah* at close range, and goes home feeling that he has fulfilled the commandment to dwell in the booth.

After the congregation has admired the *Succah,* and has "dwelt" in it, the fruits and vegetables are dismantled and taken to hospitals as a gift from the sisterhood of the congregation.

The *Succah* itself is left standing until the eighth day, at which time the concluding service of the holiday is held. On this day the Rabbi has read the final passage from the *Torah,* completing the cycle of the year's reading. Now the congregation is ready to begin anew the reading of the Torah from Creation. Therefore, on this last day of *Succoth,* two Torahs are used. From one is read the last passage

41. The modern streamlined architecture of the pulpit suggests this restrained decoration for the *Succoth* and Consecration service. Traditional harvest colors predominate. *Courtesy, Collingwood Avenue Temple, Toledo, Ohio.*

of Deuteronomy, from the other is read the first passage from Genesis, "In the beginning God created heaven and earth." Thus is there never any break in the reading of the Torah, from one religious year to another.

In the Conservative and Orthodox synagogues there is observed the ninth day of *Succoth, Simchas Torah,* the Rejoicing of the Law. In Reform temples this ninth day is combined with the services of the eighth day and the spirit of rejoicing in the Law is expressed in that service. This joy in the Law which now will be read all over again from Genesis on the Sabbath following *Succoth,* is beautifully expressed in the following poem from the Gaonic period in Babylon (from the *Service of the Synagogue,* translated by I. Zangwill) :

42. The *Succah* represents a frail dwelling place at the time of the harvest festival. Hence this *Succah,* with its delicate arrangement of branches and fruits, is symbolic of the pilgrim's offering at the end of the growing season. *Courtesy, Temple Beth Or, Montgomery, Ala.*

43. The slanting rays of the setting sun shine through the roof of the synagogue's permanent outdoor *Succah.* "The season of our gladness" is expressed by the abundance of fruits, vegetables, branches, palms and flowers. Displayed on the reception table among the trailing vines and pompons are the silver Torah crowns, a Bible, a *tallis,* a *yarmelke,* a *Shofar,* and the significant *lulav* and *etrog. Courtesy, B'nai Israel Congregation, Pittsburgh, Pa.*

This Feast of the Law all your gladness display,
    Today all your homages render.
What profit can lend one so pleasant a way,
    What jewels can vie with its splendour?
Then exult in the Law on its festival day,
    The Law is our Light and Defender.

My God I will praise in a jubilant lay,
    My hope in Him never surrender,
His glory proclaim where His chosen sons pray,
    My Rock all my trust shall engender.
Then exult in the Law on its festival day,
    The Law is our Light and Defender.

My heart of Thy goodness shall carol alway,
    Thy praises I ever will render;
While breath is, my lips all Thy wonders shall say,
    Thy truth and Thy kindness so tender.
Then exult in the Law on its festival day,
    The Law is our Light and Defender.

44. For the *Succoth* buffet table, a tall container holds a candle and dainty flowers and leaves. High arrangements are an excellent bit of technique for buffet tables since they do not interfere with the platters of food and other accoutrements. The flowers in such an arrangement must be small, as here, or the graceful line is pulled out of balance and the design appears top heavy. *Arranged by Rae L. Goldson, Woodmere, N.Y.*

CHAPTER SIX

Thanksgiving

A NATIONAL FESTIVAL

THE FOURTH OF JULY, Washington's Birthday, and Thanksgiving are celebrated by all American families whatever be their religious affiliations. They are not a part of the Jewish religious year and therefore neither the Fourth of July nor Washington's Birthday will be dealt with in this book. An exception might be made with regard to Thanksgiving.

The Puritan settlers of New England may be described as an Old Testament people. They read the Old Testament earnestly and even selected some of the laws of the Torah with which to govern their colonies.

On the basis of the biblical *Succoth,* the Feast of the Harvest, they established in the new world the harvest festival of Thanksgiving. The first such celebration took place in Plymouth, Massachusetts, in the year 1621.

It took many years before this became a widespread observance all over what later became the United States of America. Presidents Washington and Madison each proclaimed one Thanksgiving, but in each instance it was a special proclamation for that particular year. Abraham Lincoln was the first President, in 1864, to proclaim the fourth Thursday of the month of November to be observed

45. Papier-mache turkeys set off a Thanksgiving show table at a table-setting program of the sisterhood. *Courtesy, Tree of Life Sisterhood, Pittsburgh, Pa. Arranged by Mrs. Ralph Kartub and Mrs. Myer Mondell.*

by the entire nation as a day of Thanksgiving. It then became an established custom, proclaimed each year by the President of the United States.

THE AMERICAN BIRD

By now, Thanksgiving, the expression of gratitude to God for the bounties of nature, is a well established American festival. Since it is of Jewish origin, although strictly speaking not one of the festivals of the Jewish religious year, we shall include it in this book.

Thanksgiving is the only national holiday which has a religious basis. In recent years the holiday has been somewhat secularized. It marks, for example, the end of the regular college football season, but essentially, Thanksgiving has remained a family festival, observed with attendance at religious services, followed by the traditional family Thanksgiving dinner.

Many varieties of plants may be used for decorating the table or the home. But rarely is there a basic change in menu. Turkey, discovered in South America, as American as corn and sweet potatoes, is the bird which graces practically every American Thanksgiving table, along with cranberries and sweet potatoes.

46. An arrangement of dried materials planned for Thanksgiving may also adorn the home throughout the winter. On a mat of natural sheet moss (styrofoam underneath) are a dried root used as a branch to lend height, blades and tassels of cornstalks, bittersweet, lotus pods and pieces of oak tree mold. The bird with the long tail provides final rhythm to the design and has Thanksgiving significance. *Arranged by Mrs. Ronald C. Zimmer, Pittsburgh, Pa.*

47. In the great American tradition, family and friends assemble to enjoy God's bounty on Thanksgiving, having given thanks earlier in the day at a religious service. The formal table for the feast is highlighted by the luxurious triangular mass of hens-and-chickens, grapes and rhododendron leaves (sprayed gold to match the gold of the china), pheasant feathers and gold candles. Natural sheet moss spread on styrofoam forms the base. *Arranged by Mrs. Ronald C. Zimmer, Pittsburgh, Pa.*

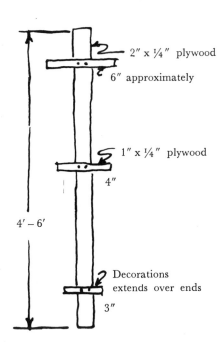

2" x ¼" plywood

6" approximately

1" x ¼" plywood

4"

4' – 6'

Decorations
extends over ends

3"

Drawing 4. Diagram of plywood used in Plate 48.
See below.

48. Strawflowers are arranged to hang gracefully against a door or wall and make an
effective decoration for the autumn festivals of
Succoth and Thanksgiving. Here, yellow, gold,
brown and moss green materials: immortelles
and glycerined viburnum leaves, are highlighted
by tin flowers. The tin flowers are cut from cans;
two or three tops, graduated in size, are placed
together for depth. Two holes are punched in
the flower and a double wire is run through,
thus forming a stem; a button center is attached.
Several thin strips of tin are cut from the sides
of the can for the tendril curls. The tin flowers,
added to the other materials, are now all assem-
bled on three separate horizontal arms. A vertical 2" x ¼" plywood strip is wrapped with 1½"
pieces of moss green felt or ribbon; then the
horizontal arms are wired in place; when the
panel is complete the looped felt bows are wired
in place. *Courtesy, Pittsburgh Garden Center.
Arranged by Mrs. Norman A. Abel.*

CHAPTER SEVEN

Chanuko,
the *Feast of Lights*

THE FESTIVAL OF HEROISM

To a child, *Chanuko* means candles and gifts. To adults this Feast of Lights means the victory of idealism over brutality, of spiritual independence over despotism, of light over darkness. *Chanuko,* a post-biblical festival, is the great festival of heroism.

It is the only holiday whose origin is precisely dated. In the year 162 before the present era, the Syrian-Greek king Antiochus ordered a pagan altar to be set in the temple in Jerusalem and sacrifices to be offered to the Greek god Zeus Olympus. A small Jewish band led by Judah Maccabeus and his brothers defied the powerful Antiochus. Fierce battles were fought, but the Jews emerged triumphant against the mighty Syrian-Greek host. The pagan altar was ripped out of the temple. The Maccabeans purified the sanctuary. The altar on which God was served was sanctified and dedicated anew. Lamps and torches were kindled as a symbol of spiritual light and freedom. The elders of Israel and Judah Maccabeus decreed a feast to be held in commemoration, a celebration of eight days. This they called *Chanuko,* the Feast of Dedication, the Festival of Lights.

49. True "*Menorah* Magic" for the *Chanuko* dinner table is created by this line-mass arrangement of green bamboo stalks and tones of lavendar gladioli and chrysanthemums, emphasized by lavendar candles. A modern effect is achieved with a plexiglass container and candlesticks placed on a structural glass plaque. *Arranged by Mrs. Manville S. Harris and Mrs. Harold M. Gup, Rochester, N. Y.*

50. A cookie door swag welcomes the children during *Chanuko*. Cookies in the shape of *dreidels* (tops) with the Hebrew letter "He" are tied with ribbons to the long-needled pine branches. The cookies, made with a special cutter, have a hole at the top for the ribbon. The pine branches are anchored on a coat hanger and chicken wire, both well concealed. The large bow at the top adds brightness; the ribboned scissors hang loose so that each visitor may cut off a cookie to enjoy. *Arranged by Mrs. Betty Berlin, Pittsburgh, Pa.*

51. Peppermint Stick *Menorah*. A delightful surprise for children is a *Menorah* sculptured from thick peppermint sticks in assorted colors. Each stick serves as a candle, the flame represented by a golden *Chanuko gelt* candy. The broad central candle is the *Shamos* light. Into this *Menorah* is placed the flower arrangement. In front of each plate is a beautifully wrapped *Chanuko* gift on top of which is a hollow *dreidel* —the top comes off and the *dreidel* is filled with gold *Chanuko gelt*. The tablecloth is made of green felt on which the gold felt star and the top have been appliqued. *Arranged by Mrs. Herbert R. Rosenthal, Pittsburgh, Pa.*

LEGENDS OF CHANUKO

In the talmudic legend we are told that when the Jews were once more in possession of the temple, they found to their dismay that all the oil in the temple had been polluted by the pagan worshippers, all except one little cruse of consecrated oil. This little cruse they nursed carefully, using it to illuminate the temple, and, miraculously, it lasted for eight days, by which time the new oil had been beaten out and prepared.

Another legend, less well known, tells of Judah and his brothers taking possession of the temple and there finding eight iron spears. On these spears, it is said, they fastened candles and lighted them, thus (says the legend) beginning the tradition of lighting the Chanuko lights.

Rabbinic law, of course, attaches importance to the lighting of the *Chanuko* lamp. It was not meant originally for the lighting of the house within, but for the illumination to shine outward so that passers-by could see it. The *Chanuko* lamps were therefore placed near the door leading to the street. If a house had more than one door, a lamp was placed in front of each. Usually as many lights were kindled as there were persons in the house. But the practice to bring the lights within the house probably began in Persia. There the fire-worshippers threatened the security of the Jews and the lamps were brought indoors.

Jewish legend was fond of connecting the heroic deeds of the biblical Judith with the Maccabean story. Hence women were bidden to light the *Chanuko* lights.

CELEBRATION IN THE HOME

Chanuko is a joyous festival, celebrated fully both in the home and in the synagogue. For the children the holiday contains two elements of surprise and delight which last throughout the eight days. There is first the ever-continuing beauty of candle lighting each day of the holiday. There is, secondly, the surprise of a new gift every evening.

In some families the father lights all the candles but the fifth. This is considered the children's candle and the youngest child is allowed to light it. And in some families the giving of *Chanuko gelt* (the tradition of gift-giving comes from the *Chanuko gelt,* money once given to poor students) occurs on the fifth night of the festival.

52. For a children's *Chanuko* party table, the central design is a large multicolored paper *dreidel* flanked by yellow chrysanthemums and eucalyptus. The *dreidels* on the napkins and plates are embossed with the Hebrew initial "He." The four sides of the die (*dreidel*) each have a letter, "Nun," "Gimel," "He" and "Shin," which are taken to be the initial letters of the sentence: "There was a great miracle there." Also, they are the special features of a game of chance, and in that capacity mean, take, half, etc., with the letter "He" standing for the word half. Paper cloth and napkins are yellow, *dreidels* on plates are yellow, on napkins, blue, to match the blue base. *Arranged by Mrs. Betty Berlin, Pittsburgh, Pa.*

53. Placed in the hallway to welcome the holiday—and the guests —this piece of sculpture with a brass *Menorah* of modern design is completed with flowers and tapers. *Arranged by Mrs. Manville S. Harris and Mrs. Harold M. Gup, Rochester, N.Y.*

But nowadays most families wisely practice the custom of spreading the gifts out over the eight days, presenting one each evening, instead of overwhelming the child with many gifts on the first night. Thus each day they have two things to look forward to, more candles to light, more gifts to receive. And in recent years books of Chanuko stories have been published, which give the children a further treat on the holiday.

54. White chrysanthemums and ti leaves are arranged in handsome bronze standards to ornament the Friday evening pulpit. The same decoration would be
suitable for *Chanuko* with a substitution of *Menorahs*. *Arranged by Mrs. Stanton
Sobel and Mrs. Robert Levy, San Francisco, Calif.*

The table is set for dinner. The *Menorah,* with its many candles which will burn all evening, occupies a position of prominence. Gift packages are heaped on the table, and the child is torn, not knowing which to do first, to open his gifts or to take part in the lighting of the candles.

The father takes into his hand the serving-light (the *Shamos*), the candle which is in the center and stands higher than the others. With this candle he will light the rest of the candles. He chants the blessings over the candles:

Blessed art Thou, O Lord our God, King of the Universe, Who has sanctified us by Thy commandment and commanded us to kindle the light of Chanuko.

Boruch atto adonoi elohenu melech ho'olom, asher kid'shonu b'mitzvosov vetzivohnu l'hadlik nayr shel Chanukah.

55. Traditional dinner setting with modern simplicity. The tapered candles, representing the *Chanuko Menorah,* are adorned with white Fuji chrysanthemums and bells of Ireland. The purple cloth and napkins are embroidered in green and pink. *Arranged by Mrs. Marcia Meyers, Pittsburgh, Pa.*

Blessed art Thou, O Lord our God, King of the Universe, Who wroughtest miracles for our fathers in days of old at this season.

Boruch atto adonoi elohenu melech ho'olom sheawsaw nisim lavosenu bayamim hawhem bazman hazeh.

And then, on the first night only, he says also the following:

Blessed art Thou, O Lord our God, King of the Universe, Who has kept us in life and has preserved us and enabled us to reach this season.

Boruch atto adonoi elohenu melech ho'olom shehecheyawnu v'kimawnu v'higyawnu lazman hazeh.

He lights the leader which in turn is used to light the other candles. In addition to the large *Menorah* which the father kindles as head of the family, in some homes each of the children has a small *Menorah* and each has the privilege of lighting the candles of his own *Menorah* and thus learning the blessings.

Then together the whole family sings the Chanuko hymn, "Rock of Ages," *Mooz Tzur*. And then, time for the presents! In time the child will learn what the holiday stands for and why we celebrate *Chanuko*. While he is small, it is enough for him to know that on this wonderful Jewish holiday we sing songs and light candles and read stories and receive beautiful presents every night for eight nights.

CELEBRATION IN THE SANCTUARY

When he goes to religious school, the child finds the whole temple or synagogue given over to the great excitement of *Chanuko*. There he learns to sing other *Chanuko* songs, make gifts for his parents. Sometimes a *Chanuko* play is

56. In a window with its view of a busy city, the Star of David rises above an unusual holiday arrangement. A beautiful *Menorah* sheds its light on flowers, fruits and prettily wrapped gifts. *Arranged by Mrs. A. L. Wolk, Pittsburgh, Pa.*

presented for the children or it may be one in which the children can participate. Sometimes there is a large celebration in which the whole school takes part.

And for adults there are services on the festival. Thus the home and the synagogue combine to give each member of the family one of the richest experiences in the religious year.

I. Peonies, rubrum lilies and buds, Persian lilacs, baptisia, Shasta daisies, nicotianas, asters, roses, hollyhocks, bleeding hearts and delphiniums are arranged in an elegant French manner. The blue, mauve, pink, rose, purple and gold of the container, a mid-eighteenth century French vase, suggest the colors used in the floral design. Set on an antique base of black and gold, and placed on a grand piano, this arrangement adds brilliance to a New Year reception. *Arranged by Mrs. Maurice Goldsmith, Pittsburgh, Pa.*

II.

III.

IV.

II. This festive dinner table suggests a harvest bounty. Two baskets, one large and one small, hold the massed grouping of a variety of chrysanthemums and dahlias, fruits, gourds, palm leaves and a miniature pottery jug, the latter two suggestive of the Holy Land. Blending candles add to the harvest coloring. The sea horse is a clever conversation piece. A rough-textured tablecloth, green plates with a grape pattern, contrasting napkins and heavy tumblers, complete the autumnal setting. *Arranged by Mrs. Robert E. Behrman, Pittsburgh, Pa.*

III. For a formal Thanksgiving luncheon, the table appointments are traditional. Oyster white linen with silver bands, Spode plates with coral borders, antique Sandwich glassware, and antique flatware—all create a true early American setting. An old Roman marble burner is placed on two wooden bases which form a two-tiered platform for the fruits and vegetables (note the blossom on the eggplant), the predominating colors being greens, dark purple, orange, rose and pink. *Arranged by Mrs. Maurice Goldsmith, Pittsburgh, Pa.*

IV. A contemporary bronze statue, "The Rabbi Holding the Torah Aloft," is by Elbert Weinberg, loaned by Mrs. Sidney A. Rosenburg. It served as center of interest for this *Bar Mitzvah* reception table in honor of the "Son of the Commandment." Rubrum lilies, tritomas, geranium leaves and podocarpus branches form the colorful crescent at the base of the figure. *Arranged by Mrs. Max Bluestone and Mrs. Herbert Schutzman, Pittsburgh, Pa.*

57. A heavy base supports a triangle of chrysanthemums and gladioli with a background of pine, all grouped around a *Menorah* on which Hebrew letters spell out *Chanuko*. To harmonize with the Torah on the *Menorah*, an antique miniature Torah rests on the base. *Arranged by Mrs. David Kirschenbaum, Harrison, N.Y.*

V. AND ON THE JACKET "Let There Be Light." Narrow tapers burning in honor of the Sabbath are a foil for spirals of eucalyptus and a few flowers. The bright red background symbolizes the warmth of Friday eve. *Arranged by Mrs. James C. Levinson, Pittsburgh, Pa.*

58. A *Chanuko* Buffet. Bronze chrysanthemums and candles are placed in a *Menorah* made of driftwood which is finished in antique white. *Arranged by Mrs. Manville S. Harris and Mrs. Harold M. Gup, Rochester, N.Y.*

CHAPTER EIGHT

The New Year for Trees

IN SOME of the American grammar schools Arbor Day and the planting of trees was a memorable observance for children. This practice is still adhered to by the Boy Scouts of America. And in the state of Israel there has been revived the old festival of *Hamishah Asar Bishebat.*

The Rabbis of the Talmud had listed three New Years for Trees: the first of *Nisan,* the first of *Tishri* and the first of *Shebat.* But the Beth Hillel (the faction which followed Hillel) decreed that the holiday was to be observed on the fifteenth of *Shebat,* hence its popular name, *Hamishah Asar Bishebat,* which means, "the fifteenth day of Shebat." This usually falls in late January or early February.

There is no special liturgy or festivity in connection with this holiday. Its observance came down mainly to the eating of many species of fruits, at least fifteen kinds and if possible those which might grow in the land of Israel. The planting of trees dates back to the time of Judah Hanassi who lived in the second century. But when the Jews were forced off the soil and away from the cultivation of the land, the holiday became merely a symbolic one and along about the sixteenth century developed into being observed merely by the eating of fruits.

59. To celebrate Arbor Day, the dinner party hostess carries out a charming plan: A tiny figure sitting atop a bowl of fruit symbolizes the planting of a tree in honor of *Hamishah Asar Bishebat.* A little tree (cut branches from her garden) is at each place and each plate is decorated with a leaf. And to "the fruit of the tree" she has added "the flowers of the field." *Arranged by Mrs. Walter Jacob, Pittsburgh, Pa.*

Now, of course, in Israel they have revived the festival. It is the school children who go out into the countryside and plant trees to make Israel a more beautiful and a more comfortable land in which to live.

We thought it would add charm to present one festival table arranged for this Arbor Day holiday, the holiday of "The New Year for Trees."

CHAPTER NINE

Purim, the Feast of Esther

THE JOY OF VICTORY

PURIM has always been the time for fun. It has been celebrated with merrymaking all through the ages. The enjoyment of laughter and play was a reaction to the misery which was overcome and the catastrophe escaped. An occasion centuries ago which might have been tragic for the Jews had a happy ending. To commemorate that joyous deliverance from the tyrant Haman, we celebrate the festival of *Purim*.

This festival has no profound religious significance. The Book of Esther, upon which it is based, does not even mention the name of God. Nor has it any connection with the harvest, as have the Pilgrim festivals. While it celebrates the rescue of the Jews from destruction by an ancient enemy, nevertheless it has none of the solemnity of the Passover which is a redemption from slavery. *Purim* indeed has in it only the element of the comic. It is in the "Guy Fawkes" tradition of poking fun at that man Haman who thought he could destroy the people whom God had declared would be eternal.

60. Early impressions are the most lasting with children, so a jolly luncheon will evoke a happy *Purim* memory. The bright linens, the spirals holding Queen Esther's crown, masks and flowers, the favors, and the clever use of carnations will delight the young folk. Of course, the *homontaschen* (Haman's pockets) are an essential delicacy. *Arranged by Mrs. J. Arthur Stein, Pittsburgh, Pa.*

THE FAST OF ESTHER

The story of *Purim* deals chiefly with certain personalities. Every child learns in religious school how to pronounce the difficult name of Ahasuerus, the king of Persia. Countless little girls for generations have enacted the role of Queen Esther in the school play. Esther, her cousin Mordecai who would not bow down to Haman, Haman the villain who was hanged from the gallows he had built for the Jews, and King Ahasuerus—these are the four personalities who held in their hands the lives of the Jews of Persia.

Haman desired the destruction of the whole of the Jewish people. To that end he purchased from Ahasuerus a
royal decree giving him permission to do with them what he
would. Mordecai, to save his people, appealed to Esther,
the queen, the only person who could plead with the king
to annul the decree.

It was not a light thing Mordecai asked. When at first
Esther might have refused, Mordecai used a persuasive

61. The bright wash of sunshine gives this *Purim* luncheon table the look
of a Dutch painting. Woven place mats of yellow and green with contrasting napkins carry out the feeling of springtime evoked by the floral
arrangement. The magnolia branch (held in the brass cup by hardware
cloth) gives the line for bright yellow daffodils placed in a dull brass tray.
One handle of the Megillah is attached by clay to the tray, the other end
is wired to the branch. *Arranged by Mrs. Sidney N. Busis and Mrs.
Bernard J. Grinberg, Pittsburgh, Pa.*

argument. He said to her: Why do you think you became the Queen of Persia? Do you not realize that God caused you to be elevated to this exalted position so that when this hour of danger came upon the people of Israel, you would be in a position to save them?

Esther begged for one day in which to make her decision. She spent that day in prayer, and in fasting. That is why the day before *Purim* is known as the Fast of Esther.

At the end of the day she appeared before the king, revealed herself as a Jewess, and pleaded for the deliverance of her people. She reminded Ahasuerus of a past service which Mordecai had rendered to the king which had gone unrewarded, and disclosed certain knowledge of past treachery on the part of Haman. Ahasuerus was moved to anger at Haman's wickedness, to regret at his ingratitude to Mordecai, to greater fondness for his queen. He annulled the decree and the people of Israel were saved.

And so on the thirteenth of Adar, the Megillah, the Scroll of Esther, is read in our temples and synagogues, giving us occasion for centuries to rejoice in the downfall of the wicked Haman and the saving of the Jews.

PURIM PLAY

Purim is celebrated in our homes in any happy way we fancy. But almost universal is the eating of one particular food which has become synonymous with *Purim*. **Mohn,** the German word for poppyseed, was associated with Homon or Haman, and a cake was fashioned long ago called *homontaschen* (haman pockets). Every years on *Purim* we eat *homontaschen*.

> 62. The Megillah is the single important symbol of *Purim*. The one used in this arrangement with spring flowers is an antique Megillah made of olive wood, widely used in Israel. In this setting we get the mood of ancient Israel and the charm of modern floral arranging. *Arranged by Mrs. James C. Levinson, Pittsburgh, Pa.*

63. *Purim* and springtime—springtime and *Purim*. The bronze cranes on either side of this arrangement—so airy it too could fly—beckon us into spring. The cycas leaves form a lace-like frame for white geraniums shown against their own lighter green leaves, on a black teak base. *Arranged by Mrs. Harry M. Aronson, Pittsburgh, Pa.*

Usually the celebrations of *Purim* are public affairs. In the religious schools plays are presented or carnivals are held for the children to which they come dressed as one of the characters in the *Purim* play. The adults too have masquerades, or dances, or parties. No matter what form our celebration takes, *Purim* is meant to be represented in the most carefree way possible.

64. To interpret music, the dance—and *Purim*—an old English crystal compote holds acacias, daffodils, irises, delphiniums, miniature eucalyptus and philodendron, repeating the colors and design of the Lenox plates. A touch of black on the plate harmonizes with the "Haman's hat" place cards. The hats (inscribed with white ink) are made from three-inch triangles of heavy black paper; the corners are rounded, pasted, and the ends are pressed together to keep them from being flat, then mounted on small pieces of styrofoam. In informal, contemporary style, the cloth is replaced by doilies, the candles omitted. *Arranged by Mrs. William H. Loveman, Shaker Heights, Ohio.*

65. Charming miniature tables for exhibition may be made for the festivals. The major difficulty is to keep everything in scale. On this *Purim* table the silver-encased Megillah set the scale. The display is complete for the basic *Purim* symbols, including the miniscule *homontaschen* and the tiny gift package. *Arranged by Mrs. Benjamin Lencher, Pittsburgh, Pa.*

66. This setting for a sisterhood program of festival tables is almost complete. Just as the program was to start, a rich mound of tiny *homontaschen* was added to candles, Haman's hat, the crown and the Megillah. *Courtesy, Tree of Life Sisterhood, Pittsburgh, Pa. Arranged by Mrs. Robert Seiavitch and Mrs. Joseph H. Tracht.*

67. The glittering crown, gilded and jeweled, is ready for Queen Esther. The
rattles (groggers) for noise, the satin fruit for luster, the flowers for springtime
—all combine to sparkle a *Purim* buffet. *Arranged by Mrs. George Goldberg,
Los Angeles, Calif.*

CHAPTER TEN

Pesach, Passover

THE MAZZOT FEAST

ALL OF LIFE re-awakens in the spring. The gardener sees the first buds, old people sigh with the joy of having come through one more winter, and every man walks with more elasticity in his step, his head raised to hear the first note of the first robin. And there is a mood of revival in our spiritual life.

Pesach has come again. It falls on the fourteenth day of the Hebrew month of *Nisan,* and it lasts, according to the Bible, for seven days. Thus Reform Judaism celebrates the festival for seven days, and Conservative and Orthodox Judaism for eight days. (This discrepancy of length of days of celebrating the festivals is explained in chapter XIV, "The Calendar.")

Passover is the oldest Jewish festival. Early in biblical days it was called the *Mazzot* Feast, the Feast of Unleavened Bread. It was connected with the pastoral life of the nomadic shepherds. Before setting out to look for new pastures for their flocks, they celebrated the arrival of another springtime by praising God and thanking Him. When this season came to praise God for these wonders of turning the hard earth into soft and pliable carpets of life-giving nour-

111

ishment, the offering which was made was the *mazzot* cake. It was a natural offering since the newly gathered barley was the staple food of the harvesters.

THE SEASON OF OUR LIBERTY

Then came danger and the struggle for survival. We surmounted the danger, we survived, we were freed from bondage. The joy of being liberated from slavery became merged with the early agricultural festival of the *Mazzot* Feast.

Passover now is called the Season of our Freedom. It is the celebration of Israel's liberation from Egyptian bondage. God commanded Moses to go forth and lead His people out of bondage. And Moses went forth, but only after a long struggle with Pharaoh was he able to obey the command to "bring the people forth out of Egypt."

Ever after we have celebrated this liberation. We rejoice anew each year at our freedom from slavery. We give thanks to God for being delivered to worship Him freely.

The ideal of freedom is hard-won and hard-kept. It is not as natural an instinct, perhaps, as that of the sweetness of life itself. So we must constantly teach it, over and over again, year after year, decade after decade, century upon century, or the world would forget. We teach this great ideal, the ideal of liberty, by telling the story of Egypt again, and again.

TELLING THE STORY

The Haggadah (the word means narrative) is the book which keeps the story alive. On the eve of the Passover we

68. An antique pewter plate with Hebrew letters spelling out *Pesach*, carnations and snapdragons, all say welcome to the holiday guests. The composition was designed for an entrance hall in the home. *Arranged by Mrs. Rinehart J. Cleary, Pittsburgh, Pa.*

celebrate the oncoming festival with a meal which we call
the *Seder*. The purpose of the *Seder* is to teach to each
new generation the story of the rigors of our slavery in
Egypt, the dangers of our escape, the joy of our liberation.
All this is contained in the Haggadah. It is a small book
because the story is easily told and can be quickly re-
counted. Since we are explaining it to children, we must

69. Three layers of matzos, the lamb bone, the bitter herbs, the *charoses*, the
wine, boiled eggs, salt water, parsley and the haggadah—all the **Pesach** symbols
—are placed before the host on this gracious *Seder* table. A personal symbol is
the small American flag which the hostess uses every year in her *Seder* arrangement. Limoges china, tall white candles blazing in antique columnar silver candlesticks, and a silver basket holding an all-white arrangement of pussywillows,
ranunculus, cyclamen, irises and stock, make an elegant composition. Elijah's
cup at the head of the table invites the prophet to the feast; he comes in spirit
while the other guests participate in actuality. *Arranged by Mrs. Aaron M. Jaffe,
Pittsburgh, Pa.*

70. Arranged for Passover is this design in the Japanese manner with pussy-willows, irises and daffodils in a black container on a black base—sharp contrast to the bright flowers. *Arranged by Mrs. Aaron M. Jaffe, Pittsburgh, Pa.*

71. "The children of Israel sang a song of praise to God by the shore of the Red Sea." To celebrate Passover, the table is set with the finest appointments, crisp linens, lighted candles and all of the meaningful symbols and foods. The antique silver basket holds freesias in varied colors, pink snapdragons and white carnations. *Arranged by Mrs. Louis Werth, San Francisco, Calif.*

describe it simply so they can understand that to be free is a blessing which all must strive to attain.

The Haggadah is decorated with beautiful pictures. It is, perhaps, the most illustrated book in Jewish literature. It is meant for the teaching of children and its simple pictures can be understood by children.

THE ORDER

The word *Seder* means order. This is a ceremonial meal and it must follow a certain order, a certain arrangement. The table must be set in a certain way. Certain special foods must be eaten. And the story of Passover must now be told. We must weave the miracle of springtime with the wonder of being freed from slavery; as much as with the text of the Haggadah do we do it with the meal itself.

On the table are the festival lamps or candles. Our best linens are used, our best silver, and we ourselves come to the feast wearing our best clothes and our best mood.

Three cakes of matzos which are folded into a napkin are placed before the father. These three cakes represent the three ancient classes in Israel, the Levites, the Cohens and the Israelites. One of the delightful customs which no household omits is the breaking of one of the pieces of matzos and hiding one half. The half which is hidden is called the *Afikomen*. This is an important symbol for the children. They know before they sit down to the meal that the *Afikomen* has been hidden by their father. They are told that whoever finds it will get a special gift. To avoid interrupting the telling of the story of Passover, the children are kept from their search for the *Afikomen* until it is time to

72. Here a beautifully illustrated Haggadah is used during Passover with an arrangement of spring flowers to set it off—irises and snapdragons and camellia foliage are artfully designed to highlight the center of interest. It may be used on a high chest, a piano, or on a mantelpiece during *Pesach,* changing the flowers when necessary. *Arranged by Mrs. Chester R. Bernstein, Pittsburgh, Pa.*

eat the meal. The *Afikomen* will be needed at the end of the meal as the final taste of matzos before the closing grace is recited. Therefore without it the service cannot be concluded.

During *Pesach* the strict command is that leaven must not be eaten throughout the seven days. It is not commanded that matzos be eaten every day, but it is commanded that it be eaten at the *Seder*. As that is a positive command, so it is a positive command that the story of Passover be told at the *Seder*.

There are four cups of wine to be drunk during the meal. Just as it is necessary to eat the matzos only at the *Seder* (but also to abstain from leaven throughout the holiday), so it is necessary only to *taste* of the four cups of wine. If it were commanded that all four cups be drained, there would be no child awake after the meal to hear the rest of the story of Passover. Only one wine cup is set before each person and that is refilled at certain stated intervals during the service.

One other cup is on the table, in front of the father. It is usually a large silver cup, or a large crystal goblet, which is filled with wine. It is the Cup of Elijah.

THE TWO ELIJAHS

There are, in our tradition, two manifestations of the Prophet Elijah. The first is the biblical Elijah, the stern prophet who brings the people from the worship of Baal to the worship of the True God. The second made his appearance in our tradition during the Middle Ages when life was so difficult for the Jews that they dreamed of the time when Elijah would come to redeem them. And so they built up around the personality of Elijah, as the agent of God's saving power, the gentle Elijah, the helper who came whenever one was in trouble and through magic or miracle

73. Although this table was set in a home, the decorations could grace the main table at a congregational *Seder*. The two high arrangements are placed on either end of the table, set in five branched silver candelabra, white candles in four of the cups; the arrangement (held in Oasis) of purple irises, white snapdragons, red and purple anemones is set in the central cup. Such a design could be used on the head table, with the low purple-and-white arrangement, flanked by pots of philodendron, placed in the center. An Haggadah could be set at each place, with the Passover symbols grouped in front of the Rabbi. A broad green satin ribbon runs the length of the table, connecting all three floral arrangements. *Arranged by Mrs. Malcolm J. Marks, Pittsburgh, Pa.*

saved and redeemed. A whole folklore thus arose centered about the figure of Elijah.

Elijah's appearance as the rescuer stems from the Prophet Malachi who, describing the great day of redemption that is to come, said: "I will send to you the Prophet Elijah who will unite the hearts of the fathers with the hearts of the children." Therefore, on this commemoration of redemption, when all the family is united at one table for worship, the door is opened and Elijah is invited as a guest and a cup of wine is prepared for him.

THE SYMBOLS OF SPRINGTIME

On a silver dish is placed a roasted lamb bone, reminiscent of the sacrificial pascal lamb which was sacrificed in Egypt. But not since those days of the temple in Jerusalem have we offered animal sacrifices to God on the altar. Therefore the roasted lamb bone is a relic, a remnant of the early days when we were turned aside from the old superstitions of pagan worship into the free-will offering of the heart of man to God.

On the same silver dish with the roasted lamb bone is the roasted egg. On Passover at the temple in Jerusalem two sacrifices were offered: one, a pascal lamb, the other, the regular holiday sacrifice as on *Shabuoth* and *Succoth*. The pascal lamb is symbolized now at the *Seder* by the lamb bone and the other sacrifice (the regular festival sacrifice) by the egg. Of course, the egg may also be taken as the symbol of the rebirth of the world in the springtime.

Then there is the root of the horseradish whose bitterness remains to remind us that the Egyptians embittered the lives of our fathers with hard labor, and the sprig of parsley which we dip into salt water, the remnant of the hyssop which was dipped into the blood of the pascal lamb to mark the door of the Hebrews in Egypt to ward off the Angel of Death.

Following all these symbols comes the *charoseth,* a compound of ground apples, raisins and almonds, mixed with cinnamon and wine. Some say that this is a symbol of the mortar which the Israelites made in building the treasure cities for Pharaoh.

The father enumerates all these symbols at the beginning of the service and explains each one as the service continues, unfolding Israel's story with each new symbol. He is assisted by the youngest child present who has the privilege of asking the Four Questions. The answers to the Four Questions give in capsule form the whole story of Passover.

74. Curved to visually encircle the *Seder* plate, this arrangement consists of fruit branches and pink and red anemones. The *Seder* plate, with Hebrew letters around the outer rim representing the *Pesach* symbols, is Israeli, as are the wooden wine bottle and wine cups (three of them mounted on wood blocks). This composition, placed on a marble base, makes for an original and colorful buffet table for any occasion at the temple during *Pesach. Courtesy, Temple Sinai, Pittsburgh, Pa. Arranged by Mrs. Mike Leebov.*

After the meal and the *benching,* the blessings or grace following the meal, certain traditional songs are sung. Chief amongst them is *Chad Gad Yo,* "A Kid, an Only Kid," which the grownups enjoy as much as the children.

Passover, coming in the spring, lends itself to a great variety of artistic displays. There is a great profusion of flowers. Flowers call to the springtime, the springtime calls to the flowers, and both call to Passover. In the season of our great deliverance, from our own Egypts as well as the Egypt of our people, we rejoice in the celebration of the *Seder* and make our tables and homes as festive as possible.

CHAPTER ELEVEN

Shabuoth, Pentecost

SHABUOTH

SHABUOTH is the Feast of Weeks, the Pentecost, which comes seven weeks, or fifty days (from whence it derives its name "Pentecost," which is the Greek word for fifty) after *Pesach*. Its original name was *Chag ha'Kotsir*, the Feast of the Harvest. While it is one of the Pilgrim festivals, in Reform Judaism it has become more significant for its historical implications. It is the time of the giving of the Law. On *Shabuoth* we celebrate the great occasion of God's gift of the Torah through Moses to Israel.

ISRAEL'S CHOICE

The story of the giving of the Law on Mount Sinai is known to everyone. The Midrash adds an interesting sidelight. When our forefathers were marching through the desert to the Promised Land, God decided that at Mount Sinai He would give them His Law. But before He "chose" the people of Israel to accept the Torah, with all its responsibilities, He first asked the other nations of the world if they would accept it so that at no time in the future would they be jealous of the children of Israel for possessing the

Torah. The children of Esau were asked, then the children of Lot, then the children of Ishmael. All the peoples of the world had the Torah offered to them but everyone refused to accept the Torah with its many commandments and strict responsibilities.

But the children of Israel accepted the Torah. Thus the theme of the Midrash seems to be that it was not so much that God chose Israel but that Israel chose God.

75. The large pulpit suggests that a large Confirmation class is being inducted into the tenets of Judaism. Therefore much free space is required on the pulpit. Consequently the floral arangements are placed at the front. White (of the flowers, in the Ark, and of the Torah covers) reminds the congregation that the service also is a celebration of a festival, and here it is the harvest festival of *Shabuoth*. The tall urns at the sides and the fan-shaped center design add a welcome contrast in height. Chrysanthemums, stocks, gladioli and snapdragons highlight the dark oak paneling. *Courtesy, Rodef Shalom Temple, Pittsburgh, Pa.*

76. A closeup of the preceding picture shows the fan-shaped arrangement and white boxes filled with chrysanthemums and lemon leaves. On the pulpit desk is the open Bible, ready for the readings from Torah and Prophets. The tables at the sides of the altar await the bouquets of the girl confirmands. *Courtesy, Rodef Shalom Temple, Pittsburgh, Pa.*

Drawing 5. First step in making the arrangement shown in Plate 77.

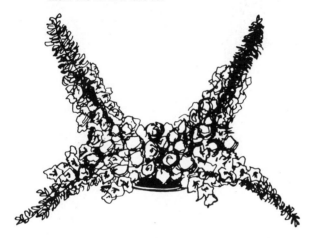

Drawing 6. Second step in making the arrangement shown in Plate 77.

77. A small sanctuary requires special treatment so as not to overpower the available space for a *Shabuoth* Confirmation service. The open Ark displays the Torahs
in ceremonial garb. Since the holiday commemorates the giving of the Law as
well as the summer harvest festival, flowers and branches outline the two tablets
of the Ten Commandments etched into the pulpit desk. The parabolic arc
arrangement is anchored in Oasis placed in a boat-shaped bowl. White gladioli
and peonies, forsythia and orange blossom greens compose this arrangement.
(Substitutes could be stocks, snapdragons, delphiniums, Shasta daisies, irises,
lilies, apple blossoms or bridal wreath.) During the service the girls' bouquets are
placed on tables at the side of the pulpit. These are charming and old-fashioned,
made with lace doilies, white satin ribbons, pompons and daisies. *Josiah and
Carrie Cohen Chapel, Rodef Shalom Temple, Pittsburgh, Pa. Arranged by Mrs.
Betty Berlin.*

78. The spirit of the sacred vows to be taken by the young confirmands is expressed in this all-white altar setting: the Torah covers, the pulpit cloth, the carpeting and the gladioli and chrysanthemums reflect the radiance of the message of consecration. *Courtesy, Collingwood Avenue Temple, Toledo, Ohio.*

CONFIRMATION

On *Shabuoth* we celebrate this great occasion, the time of the giving of the Law, and we ask our children, who are being confirmed, to dedicate themselves, too, to the Torah. Reform Judaism instituted Confirmation at the beginning of the nineteenth century. It differed from the older *Bar Mitzvah* in three ways: First, the ceremony of dedication takes place once a year instead of many times a year at each individual's *Bar Mitzvah;* secondly, therefore, it was a Confirmation of an entire class and not merely of an individual; and thirdly, it completed the evolution of the high status of women already inherent in Judaism. It declared the full equality of men and women and gave this modern *Bar Mitzvah* to both.

Nowadays, Conservative Judaism, and also certain groups of Neo-Orthodoxy have adopted a Confirmation service for their young people fashioned after the service developed by Reform Judaism.

79. **This pulpit in a large temple requires the elaborate display of flowers and greens to emphasize the formality of a Confirmation service. The *Shabuoth* mood is expressed by the use of white gladioli, carnations and apple blossoms along with rhododendron branches and trailing ivy. The flowers and greens banked in an arch at the sides form a handsome setting for the imposing arch of the pulpit.** *Courtesy, Congregation Rodeph Sholom, New York, N.Y.*

80. The Confirmation day luncheon table centerpiece, done in the oriental manner, is placed on a large base with a bronze container featuring miniature red
roses and grape ivy, plus a group of Confirmation certificates. A Bible is placed
at the head of the table. White cut-work linens repeat the filigree look of the
china plates. *Arranged by Mrs. Harry M. Aronson, Pittsburgh, Pa.*

Confirmation was at first not placed on *Shabuoth*. Some thought it would be suitable on *Succoth*, some on Passover. But very soon it was *Shabuoth* which was selected. *Shabuoth*, the time of Israel's acceptance of the Law, became the ideal time for Confirmation, the time of the children's acceptance of religious responsibilities. Since Israel was on this day "confirmed" into its faith by Moses, so we, each year, confirm our children into their faith.

FESTIVAL OF FIRST FRUITS

The agricultural nature of *Shabuoth* was expressed all through the Middle Ages even when the Jews lived in the ghettoes of Europe and other lands. The synagogue was decorated with green branches on this festival, and we today at our Confirmation in Reform and Conservative temples and synagogues always express our praise of the earth and its life-giving and beautifying qualities with lavish use of floral decorations. Our sanctuaries are decorated

81. The "stone" tablets of the Law are easy to make. These pictured here, to represent the giving of the Law on Mount Sinai, are of cardboard, painted gray, the Hebrew letters of the commandments heavily inked for sharpness. The harvest character of the festival is carried out with the spring flowers and the "first" grapes. It is a natural setting for a celebration of the acceptance of religious responsibility and is suitable for Confirmation afternoon or for a springtime or summertime *Bar* or *Bath Mitzvah. Arranged by Mrs. Herbert Jacobson, Pittsburgh, Pa.*

with green branches and flowers. In the Confirmation service the girls carry flowers which are used during an impressive flower prayer in which all the girls participate.

During the *Shabuoth* services in the temple and synagogue the Book of Ruth is read. This book contains some of the most beautiful words found in the Bible. The Moabite woman would have found life amongst her own people easier, but, upon the death of her husband, when his mother, Naomi, prepared to return to her own people, Ruth pleaded for permission to accompany her. Naomi warned her of the difficulties of coming to a strange people. But Ruth insisted, and spoke the famous and inspiring words: "Whither thou goest, I shall go. Thy people shall be my people, thy God my God."

In this Book also is a description of the scene of harvesting. Thus the Book of Ruth, which speaks of her reaping of the harvest and her acceptance of Judaism, is appropriate to the festival of the Law and of the harvest.

With *Shabuoth,* the chief festivals of the Jewish year come to a close.

82. An unusual use of a Torah crown, to symbolize the giving of the Law on Mount Sinai, appropriate for Confirmation, the time of the taking of religious vows. The crown is set in the central holder of the five-branched candelabrum to tower over the floral arrangement of pink azaleas and white candytuft (placed in Oasis and wired to each of the four holders), with nosegays of smaller azaleas at the base. The silver place plates with the silver candelabrum and the silver Torah crown, and the embroidered pink organdy cloth with the pink azaleas, make a dignified and gracious composition. *Arranged by Mrs. Joel Spear, Jr., and Mrs. David Weill, Jr., Pittsburgh, Pa.*

83. For a Confirmation buffet table, yellow roses are woven around the bronze figurines which are encircled by grape ivy. Height in the composition is achieved by the lines of the bells of Ireland and tall white candles. Other flowers may replace the roses: pink camellias, rose-colored azaleas, red tulips, purple anemones. The wallpaper of the dining room dictates the use of flowers in mauve hues. *Arranged by Mrs. Gilbert S. Broff, Pittsburgh, Pa.*

84. There is a duality in *Shabuoth:* one side deals with the ceremony of Confirmation, the other side reveals the elementary feature of the harvest season. Sprays of barley, lemons and garden petunias are combined with the short broad candles, cleverly placed on inverted wine glasses. The bare oak table top makes an intriguing modern setting for the black place plates and gleaming amber crystal. *Arranged by Mrs. James C. Levinson, Pittsburgh, Pa.*

CHAPTER TWELVE

Bar and Bath Mitzvah, the Son and Daughter of the Commandment

PERSONAL FESTIVITIES

UP TO THIS POINT this book has dealt with the religious observances of the congregation. But there are two celebrations which are highly individualized, that of *Bar* and *Bath Mitzvah,* and Marriage. These occasions do not belong primarily to the community but to the individual family. Furthermore they do not commemorate a religious festival but rather a religious ceremony involving one, or two people. However, these ceremonies of *Bar* and *Bath Mitzvah* and of weddings are so much a part of personal and religious experience that they must be included in a book dealing with floral arrangements for religious occasions in our life.

BAR MITZVAH

RIGHTS AND DUTIES

By tradition the age of thirteen marks the beginning of religious responsibility. A special ceremony, the ceremony of *Bar Mitzvah,* marks this assumption of maturity. After his *Bar Mitzvah* ceremony the boy may wear the phylacteries (the *tefillin*) and has the right to be called up for the read-

Drawing 7. A step in making the arrangement shown in Color Plate IV.

ing of the Torah. He is now counted in the *minyan* of ten men, the quorum, for religious services and possesses all the religious rights and duties of a grown man.

THE CEREMONY

The *Bar Mitzvah* ceremony contains three parts.

BARUCH SHEPETARANI

On the Sabbath or festival following a boy's thirteenth

birthday, the boy and his family and friends come to the synagogue or temple. At the appropriate time in the service the boy and his father join the Rabbi on the pulpit. The father recites the following blessing:

> *Boruch shefsawrani mayawnsho shel zeh.*
> Blessed be He Who hath freed me from the responsibility of this child.

The father has thus shed his religious responsibility for his son; his son now assumes those responsibilities. He is given the privilege that day of reading the weekly portion, the Sedra, from the Torah, and also of reading the Haftorah portion, from the Prophets.

THE DERASHAH

The *Bar Mitzvah* boy then makes his address to the congregation. This is followed by the address of the Rabbi to the boy and the blessing over the boy by the Rabbi.

THE SE'UDAH

In olden days the address of the *Bar Mitzvah* boy was presented at the festive meal in celebration of the occasion, the *Se'udah*. Today the address is part of the religious service of the day. After the services, the family and friends may retire to the vestry room or social hall for light refreshments, or for a formal luncheon. Or the luncheon or dinner or reception may take place in a hotel or a club or at home.

85. Suitable for any *Bar* or *Bath Mitzvah* party, in synagogue or temple, or in the home. The Spanish figure, with the Ten Commandments etched in Hebrew, becomes the focal point for the arrangement of sansevieria and philodendron foliage, and gladioli blossoms, all set on slate. *Arranged by Temple Shalom Garden Club of West Newton, Mass.*

BATH MITZVAH

A New Development

Although technically speaking a woman cannot be counted
to the *minyan* (the quorum) in traditional Judaism, nevertheless in America a ceremony for girls has been developed
paralleling *Bar Mitzvah*. This really is a recognition of the
increasingly important role that a woman plays in every
branch of Jewish religious life. Although there are many
strict Orthodox authorities who say, with technical correct-
ness, that the ceremony can have no meaning and is therefore unauthorized, nevertheless *Bath Mitzvah* has become
increasingly popular in Conservative, some Reform, and

86. For a *Bar* or *Bath Mitzvah,* a modern pulpit is decorated with large white
chrysanthemums and mixed foliage in white containers echoing the white marble
surrounding the Ark. *Courtesy, Tree of Life Synagogue, Pittsburgh, Pa.*

87. An especially attractive feature of this table for a *Bar Mitzvah* dinner is the centerpiece made of several small containers grouped together. After dinner, each young lady guest may take home one small arrangement. The flowers are in deep masculine tones—dark blue anemones, purple heather and red carnations, with white carnations and deutzia to match the container. Gold-rimmed place plates pick up the gold of the fern motif in the cloth; the blue of the anemones repeats the blue of the plates. *Arranged by Mrs. William H. Loveman, Shaker Heights, Ohio.*

some modern Orthodox congregations. This is a very new ceremony only developed in recent years and is not as yet too widespread.

THE CELEBRATION

The *Bath Mitzvah* ceremony is usually held on the Friday evening closest to the girl's twelfth birthday. She participates in the service at the temple or synagogue, reading the Haftorah portion (and in Reform congregations, the Torah portion), and gives a little address to the Congregation. To her too the Rabbi gives his blessing, and a brief address. After the services the congregation is invited by the girl's parents to the *Oneg Shabbat* which is in the girl's honor. That evening before services there may have been a dinner in her honor; or, on the next day, a luncheon or an afternoon reception may be a celebration for the *Bath Mitzvah* girl.

88. For a *Bar Mitzvah* reception this asymmetrical design of pink asters, darker heather, yew, pachysandra and spring branches, is placed on a double base; a boy's heirloom Bible completes the design for a side table. *Arranged by Mrs. Ronald C. Zimmer, Pittsburgh, Pa.*

89. "Thou shalt love the Lord thy God, with all thy heart and with all thy soul and with all thy might . . . " *V'ohavto es adonoi elohecho*. The paragraph following the *Sh'ma Yisroel* in Deuteronomy VI and in all the prayerbooks, Reform, Conservative and Orthodox, is the section chosen by the artist who made the scroll and also designed the table especially for this *Bar Mitzvah* reception. *Courtesy of Mr. and Mrs. Irwin Miller, Pass-A-Grille Beach, St. Petersburg, Fla. Designed by Mrs. Benjamin Lencher, Pittsburgh, Pa.*

90. This attractive setting for a *Bar Mitzvah Oneg Shabbat* at temple or synagogue keeps to a blue-and-white motif, with a variety of textures to compensate for the monochrome. The birds shade from light, to medium, to dark blue, the flowers, from very light to deep blue. White flowers and light greens add interest. *Arranged by Mrs. George Goldberg, Los Angeles, Calif.*

91. Matching arrangements feature several varieties of chrysanthemums and snapdragons artfully arranged in structural harmony with the modernistic pulpit. This arrangement may be used as well for any Sabbath service; here we honor the *Bath Mitzvah* girl. *Arranged by Temple Shalom Garden Club of West Newton, Mass.*

92. The serious part of the ceremony of *Bath Mitzvah* at temple or synagogue is over, and the young girl may now enjoy the party in her home. This original and charming arrangement centers on a pretty doll and her pretty hat. It is sure to enchant the early adolescent. Roses may be used at any season, and lilies-of-the-valley and azaleas or violets or forget-me-nots or sweet peas, with foliage for a background. *Arranged by Mrs. Benjamin Mallinger and Mrs. Sidney A. Silverman, Pittsburgh, Pa.*

93. A *Bath Mitzvah* is a personal event so it may be celebrated with the girl's best friends as luncheon guests. The pink rose pattern in the plates suggests the rose-decorated cake, ribbons of pastel shades, and the airy topiary "tree" of dainty pink and white flowers—miniature carnations, snowflake chrysanthemums and snapdragons. *Arranged by Mrs. Melvin J. Levine, Pittsburgh, Pa.*

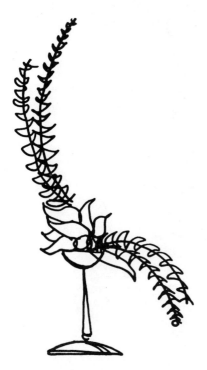

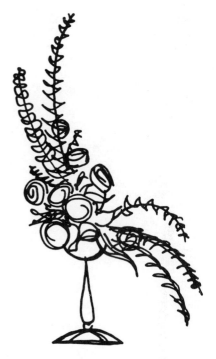

Drawing 8. First step in making the arrangement shown in Plate 94.

Drawing 9. Second step in making the
arrangement shown in Plate 94.

94. This arrangement begins with the filigree base of an inverted silver compote,
used as a container (with Oasis holding the flowers), and the miniature antique
Torah. The graceful sweep of the looped and pointed dracaena leaves, the pink
miniature roses and the heather form a picture for any spot in the festive home
to celebrate a *Bath Mitzvah. Arranged by Mrs. Cuddy Briskin, Pittsburgh, Pa.*

95. The last of the autumn fruits and flowers provide a gracious mass arrangement for a fall *Bath Mitzvah*. This design would be suitable also for any of the autumn festivals. *Arranged by Mrs. Edward Lee, Scarsdale, N.Y.*

96. Bronze gladioli and Rex begonia leaves (placed in a pinholder inserted in the top of the container) are suitably blended with family heirlooms—a brass samovar and candlesticks—to form an appealing composition for a *Bath Mitzvah Oneg Shabbat* following the services in the synagogue or temple. *Arranged by Mrs. Manville S. Harris and Mrs. Harold M. Gup, Rochester, N.Y.*

ᴍarriage

"THE BUILDING OF JOY"

IN RABBINIC LITERATURE wedded life was looked upon as the most natural, and the most exalted state. The Rabbis described the unmarried man as living without joy, without blessing and without good. And so they counselled: One should first establish a home, and plant a vineyard, and then, marry.

In Judaism marriage is not primarily a rite. It is a mutual contract, of such supreme importance that it is given the title of sanctification, *kiddushin*. Rabbinic laws place around marriage certain safeguards and these safeguards are contained in a *Ketuba*, a contract. This *Ketuba*, this contract, possesses not merely a mundane character natural to all contracts, but it possesses particularly a special religious character. The formula of marriage is purely legal, but in Judaism it is surrounded by benedictions invoking the blessing of God and His sanction.

Since marriage means the founding of a home, it is naturally observed with pomp and ceremony. It is surrounded with festivity and with joy.

97. Australia's national flower, the Waratah, now being imported into the United States, is used here on a formal reception table to announce an engagement. The white bisque figures are highlighted by two bright red flowers, flanked by unusual twisted white candles. *Arranged by Mrs. Gilbert Goldman, Pittsburgh, Pa.*

THE MARRIAGE CEREMONY

Jewish marriage, whether Orthodox, Conservative or Reform, varies little in its basic elements. The traditional ceremony first brings the bridal pair under the *Chuppah*. Then follows the benediction of espousal over the first cup of wine from which the bride and groom drink. The groom then places the ring on the left hand of the bride and recites the espousal formula:

> *Harayat mekedeshes li b't'bas zu k'das Moshe v'Yisroel.*
> Be thou consecrated unto me according to the laws of Moses and Israel.

The *Ketuba* (the marriage contract) is then read. This is followed by the benediction over the second cup of wine

98. A white satin Bible and a delicate spray of orchids make a fitting decoration for a tea for the bride. Gracefully feminine, this arrangement is appropriate for any occasion honoring a bride or bride-to-be. *Arranged by Mrs. Louis J. Hoechstetter, Pittsburgh, Pa.*

99. Pink roses in a white cupid vase harmonize with the pink-and-white floral wallpaper and the lamps with smaller cupids. This arrangement is calculated to charm the bride as she dresses for her wedding. *Courtesy, Rodef Shalom Temple, Pittsburgh, Pa. Arranged by Mrs. James H. Rich.*

from which the couple drinks also. Then follow the other marriage benedictions, the *Sheba Berachoth,* the Seven Blessings.

These basic parts of the ceremony are accompanied by various embellishments, such as a speech, processions and similar expansions to lend pomp and dignity to the ceremony.

Reform Judaism shortens the ceremony and often in a Reform wedding the *Chuppah* is not used, nor is the glass broken. But the espousal formula and the use of the wedding ring are common to all Jewish religious ceremonies of marriage.

Based upon the precedent of an incident in the **Bible,** the custom arose in medieval times of breaking a glass at

100. The candles and ferns surrounding the pulpit make a frame for the altar decoration composed of madonna lilies, gerberas and Fuji chrysanthemums. An airy design which does not overpower even a small chapel decorated for a wedding. *Courtesy of Mrs. Milton Male. Josiah and Carrie Cohen Chapel, Rodef Shalom Temple, Pittsburgh, Pa.*

101. For a June wedding, here is a more elaborate decoration in the same chapel as in the preceding illustration. Here lily-decked standards at the pews, a floral arch and flowered trellises are the materials. *Krause-Pirchesky Wedding. Josiah and Carrie Cohen Chapel, Rodef Shalom Temple, Pittsburgh, Pa.*

the ceremony. The Sephardic Jews broke the glass in the middle of the ceremony and when it was broken the people present recited the verse: "If I forget thee, O Jerusalem, may my right hand forget its cunning." Among the Ashkenazic Jews, the custom developed to break the glass at the end of the ceremony, at which time no one particularly observed the custom of reciting the Bible verse, but merely cried out *Mazel Tov, Mazel Tov,* "Good luck, Good luck."

THE CHUPPAH

The origin of the wedding canopy (the *Chuppah*), a tapestry on four poles, whose use is so widespread, has the air of very ancient custom. Probably our present use dates from the sixteenth century. Some scholars say the *Chuppah* means the retiring of the couple to privacy, others that the mere bringing of the bride into the groom's house for the purpose of marriage was called *Chuppah*. Some say it means the spreading of the *tallith* (the prayer shawl) over the bride's head during the reciting of the blessing.

In our time it is clear that *Chuppah* is the place where a cloth is put over four poles and there the couple comes to be united in marriage.

102. The chapel decorations shown in preceding photograph now adorn the bride's table in the Solomon B. Freehof Hall, Rodef Shalom Temple, Pittsburgh. *Krause-Pirchesky Wedding.*

103. Modern architecture for synagogues, having strong geometric lines, requires restrained decoration. Here a few flowers and candles, shown against ferns, are effective in their simplicity. *Liff-Hurwitz Wedding. Deaktor Chapel, B'Nai Israel Synagogue, Pittsburgh, Pa.*

WEDDING FLOWERS

Perhaps it is at weddings that flowers are most lavishly used. There are, of course, many weddings where the floral decorations are kept simple. But usually restraint is removed, and the air of a wedding is fragrant with the scent of many blooms.

104. The bridal table is effective in front of the draperies in the social hall of the synagogue. The fountain, decorated with white flowers and ferns, stands about two feet in front of the wedding table. On the bride's table are tiered fruit decorations, a centerpiece of white carnations and garlands of southern smilax. *Gordon-Schachter Marriage at Pittsburgh, Pa.*

105. There is imagery in this garden setting created for the marriage altar. A small picket fence defines the boundaries, matting on the floor simulates grass, and ferns in the corners represent trees. *Courtesy of Rabbi and Mrs. Aaron I. Ilson. Falk Auditorium, Temple Sinai, Pittsburgh, Pa.*

107. After the marriage, the *Chuppah*, flanked by novel pyramids of flowers, became part of the decorations in the dining room. Because of the elaborate floral arrangements and the abundant use of greens, the *Chuppah* of necessity was kept simple. *Zeiden-Kleban Wedding, Pittsburgh, Pa.*

106. A pleasing triangular effect leads the eye from the mass arrangements in the background to the candelabra and on to the low centerpiece which trails partly over the table edge. *Kaufman-Friedlander Wedding. Beth Shalom Synagogue, Pittsburgh, Pa.*

108 and 109. This *Chuppah* will also become the central decoration for the bride's table. After the wedding ceremony has been performed, the wedding party and guests are on the receiving line in another room; then the bridal table is set up in front of the *Chuppah*. Ferns are placed to conceal the two steps which lead to the altar. The chairs for the bride and groom are placed at the table directly in front of the *Chuppah*, and on the table a floral centerpiece completes the ornate candle-fountain-floral display. *Ruben-Glick Wedding, Pittsburgh, Pa.*

110. Following the marriage ceremony in the chapel, the wedding party received the guests here. The borders of the garden court were decorated with yellow gladioli among the permanent plantings of evergreens and ivy. On the dais was placed a profusion of ferns, giving an airy setting for the antique bronze *Menorah* which was used as the center of interest in the outdoor decorations. *Courtesy of Mrs. Irving F. Levitt. Marcus Aaron Garden Court, Rodef Shalom Temple, Pittsburgh, Pa.*

111. There is nothing old-fashioned about this contemporary arrangement of white anthuriums, ferns, dracaena and ti leaves designed for a silver anniversary buffet table. Silver birds are important to the design and have symbolic importance too! *Arranged by Mrs. Cuddy Briskin, Pittsburgh, Pa.*

Drawing 10. Basic step for arrangement shown in Plate 111.

112. Arranged for a golden anniversary celebration in the garden. The huge leaf at the base of the figure gives balance to the arrangement of yellow Fuji chrysanthemums, carnations and irises, green bells of Ireland, podocarpus leaves and ferns. The full flower mass, with a golden "50" tucked among the blooms, and an abundance of fruits topped by another golden "50," testify to a life blessed by long years. *Arranged by Mrs. James A. Frank, Pittsburgh, Pa.*

CHAPTER FOURTEEN

The Calendar

THE DAY

THE BIBLE, in Genesis, sets down the boundaries for the Jewish day: "And there was evening and there was morning one day." The Jewish day begins at sunset and ends at sunset. To limit the observance of the Day of Atonement in Leviticus we read: "From even unto even." There is a guiding rule for knowing when the evening actually starts: When three stars can be seen in the sky, then is the evening begun.

DAY NAMES

The Sabbath (and Friday, which is known as *Erev Shabbos*) is the only day which is named in the Jewish calendar. Sunday is called "the first day," Monday "the second," etc. In ancient times Monday and Thursday were market days and people came into the cities from the farm lands. They also became the days when the courts convened. So too in the synagogues those mornings became special occasions. Since so many people were gathered, special prayers and special observances were held on Mondays and Thursdays.

WEEK NAMES

It was the Jews who introduced into the Roman world the idea of grouping the days into weeks, in periods of seven. This was later adopted by the Christians. The Babylonians probably originated the idea of the week because of the four phases of the moon, the new moon, the first quarter, the full moon, and the third quarter. These are, roughly, seven days apart. In ancient times the seventh day was considered unlucky until Judaism gave it a sacred character and made of it a holy day of rest.

Although only Friday and Saturday have names in the Jewish calendar, the weeks do have names. They developed from the portion of the Torah read at the religious services. For example, there is the week called "the Sabbath of Genesis," or, the week called "the Sabbath of Noah," etc. The prophetic portions which are read at the services have given names to some Sabbaths, such as "the Sabbath of Comfort." The reading which that week comes from is the fortieth chapter of Isaiah which begins with the words: "Comfort ye, comfort ye, My people." Other Sabbaths have special names derived from special readings or observances. The Sabbath before Passover is one such, and is called "the Great Sabbath." So also the Sabbath before Purim is called "the Sabbath of 'Remember'" because of the special reading, "Remember Amalek."

LUNAR CALENDAR

The Hebrew month is lunar, as were the months in all ancient calendars. The month is counted from new moon to new moon, or approximately twenty-nine and a half days. Since a month cannot begin in the middle of a day, a lunar month is either twenty-nine days or thirty days. The court (the *Sanhedrin*) in olden times determined whether the month should consist of twenty-nine or thirty days by requiring people who saw the new moon to come before them and testify that they saw it. If the court were satisfied, they then proclaimed that day to be the new moon and the beginning of the next month. Signal fires were then lighted on the mountaintops to inform the people of the rise of the new moon. The people would thus know when to observe the festivals.

Those people who lived far from Palestine could not, of course, see the fires on the tops of the mountains and could not be certain when the new moon began. Therefore they could not know the exact day of a festival. Since, however, there was a doubt only about one day (whether the preceding month contained twenty-nine or thirty days), in order to celebrate the festivals without falling into error, they simply added one day to the festivals. Thus Passover was observed in Palestine for seven days, but outside of Palestine it became the custom to celebrate the festival for eight days.

MATHEMATICAL CALENDARS

By the third century of our era calendars became fixed by mathematical and astronomic calculations. There no longer was room for doubt as to when a new month began and the lighting of bonfires on mountaintops ceased. However, the Jews living outside of Palestine never reverted to the Palestinian custom of celebrating the festival of Passover for seven days, or of *Shabuoth* for one day, until modern times when the Reform Jews did revert to the Palestinian custom.

MONTH NAMES

In ancient days the months were merely called "the first month," "the second month," etc. Traces of ancient names are retained in the Bible: the name *Oviv* for springtime, *Ziv,* for the second month, *Esonim,* for the seventh month, and *Bul,* for the eighth month. After the people of Israel came back to Palestine from the Babylonian exile, it became customary to name the months. These names are still used in the Jewish calendar: *Nison, Iyor, Sivon, Tamuz, Ov, Elul, Tishri, Cheshvon, Kislev, Tebet, Sh'vot, Adar.*

LEAP YEAR

A dislocation occurs in the year because the Hebrew calendar is lunar. Twelve months of twenty-nine and one-half days amount to a year of three hundred and fifty-four days. This is eleven and one-half days short of the sun year. After three years of twelve lunar months the moon year would be thirty-three days (or more than a month) behind the sun year. If the lunar calendar were not corrected, the festivals would be dislocated. Passover, a spring festival, would, after three years, come in the wintertime. The seasons depend upon the sun year and the moon year had to correspond. It was this need for keeping religious festivals at the right season which led to the correction of the lunar calendar among all peoples.

In ancient days a practical method was used to determine whether it was necessary to add an extra month in a particular year. The barley harvest, the earliest of the grains to ripen, was usually ripe by Passover. The officials would go out to the fields and judge the state of the crops. If they saw that it was impossible for the barley to be ripe by Passover, they knew that the calendar was behind the sun year, and they added an extra month. The next new moon therefore was declared to be not *Nisan* but "the Second *Adar.*" Nowadays the leap year is determined mathematically. In a group of nineteen years the leap month, the Second *Adar,* is added seven times. When there is a leap year, the festival of *Purim* is celebrated in the Second *Adar.*

THE CALENDAR

In the Jewish Prayerbook the new year begins on the first of *Tishri* which is called "The New Year for Years." This is the "religious year," and the one we follow in this festival and flower book.

Tishri first	New Year
Tishri tenth	Day of Atonement
Tishri fifteenth	Succoth
Kislev twenty-fifth	*Chanuko*
Adar fourteenth	*Purim*
2nd *Adar* in Leap Years, the fourteenth	*Purim*
Nison fifteenth	Passover
Sivon sixth	*Shabuoth*

There are exactly forty-nine days, or seven weeks, from the second day of Passover to *Shabuoth,* the Feast of Weeks. *Shabuoth* therefore always occurs one day later in the week than the first day of Passover. There are ten days between the New Year and the Day of Atonement. Thus the Day of Atonement always comes two days later in the week than the New Year. Since there is also a rule that the New Year can never occur on Sunday, Wednesday, or Friday, the Day of Atonement, which is two days later in the following week, cannot occur on Tuesday, Friday or Sunday.

From the time of the Maccabees and until about the twelfth century, the Jews used the era of Seleucus, the successor of Alexander in western Asia, for dating documents. It became known in Jewish literature as the year of Deeds. The era now in use became prevalent about the twelfth century and refers back, traditionally, to the creation of the world.

A 25-Year Calendar

All holidays begin on the eve before the indicated date.

	Rosh Hashonah	Yom Kippur	Succoth	Chanuko	Purim	Passover	Shabuoth
1964-65	Sept. 7	Sept. 16	Sept. 21	Nov. 30	Mar. 18	Apr. 17	June 6
1965-66	Sept. 27	Oct. 6	Oct. 11	Dec. 19	Mar. 6	Apr. 5	May 25
1966-67	Sept. 15	Sept. 24	Sept. 29	Dec. 8	Mar. 26	Apr. 25	June 14
1967-68	Oct. 5	Oct. 14	Oct. 19	Dec. 27	Mar. 14	Apr. 13	June 2
1968-69	Sept. 23	Oct. 2	Oct. 7	Dec. 16	Mar. 4	Apr. 3	May 23
1969-70	Sept. 13	Sept. 22	Sept. 27	Dec. 5	Mar. 22	Apr. 21	June 10
1970-71	Oct. 1	Oct. 10	Oct. 15	Dec. 23	Mar. 11	Apr. 10	May 30
1971-72	Sept. 20	Sept. 29	Oct. 4	Dec. 13	Feb. 29	Mar. 30	May 19
1972-73	Sept. 9	Sept. 18	Sept. 23	Dec. 1	Mar. 18	Apr. 17	June 6
1973-74	Sept. 27	Oct. 6	Oct. 11	Dec. 20	Mar. 8	Apr. 7	May 27
1974-75	Sept. 17	Sept. 26	Oct. 1	Dec. 9	Feb. 25	Mar. 27	May 16
1975-76	Sept. 6	Sept. 15	Sept. 20	Nov. 29	Mar. 16	Apr. 15	June 4
1976-77	Sept. 25	Oct. 4	Oct. 9	Dec. 17	Mar. 4	Apr. 3	May 23
1977-78	Sept. 13	Sept. 22	Sept. 27	Dec. 5	Mar. 23	Apr. 22	June 11
1978-79	Oct. 2	Oct. 11	Oct. 16	Dec. 25	Mar. 13	Apr. 12	June 1
1979-80	Sept. 22	Oct. 1	Oct. 6	Dec. 15	Mar. 2	Apr. 1	May 21
1980-81	Sept. 11	Sept. 20	Sept. 25	Dec. 3	Mar. 20	Apr. 19	June 8
1981-82	Sept. 29	Oct. 8	Oct. 13	Dec. 21	Mar. 9	Apr. 8	May 28
1982-83	Sept. 18	Sept. 27	Oct. 2	Dec. 11	Feb. 27	Mar. 29	May 18
1983-84	Sept. 8	Sept. 17	Sept. 22	Dec. 1	Mar. 18	Apr. 17	June 6
1984-85	Sept. 27	Oct. 6	Oct. 11	Dec. 19	Mar. 7	Apr. 6	May 26
1985-86	Sept. 16	Sept. 25	Sept. 30	Dec. 8	Mar. 25	Apr. 24	June 13
1986-87	Oct. 4	Oct. 13	Oct. 18	Dec. 27	Mar. 15	Apr. 14	June 3
1987-88	Sept. 24	Oct. 3	Oct. 8	Dec. 16	Mar. 3	Apr. 2	May 22
1988-89	Sept. 12	Sept. 21	Sept. 26	Dec. 4	Mar. 21	Apr. 20	June 9
1989-90	Sept. 30	Oct. 9	Oct. 14	Dec. 23	Mar. 11	Apr. 10	May 30

CHAPTER FIFTEEN

The Science of Flower Arranging

THROUGHOUT THIS BOOK, flowers are shown arranged in various styles. Some are traditional, a number are oriental, and a fair proportion are contemporary or modern. All of them are *designed*—they are composed according to aesthetic principles. These aesthetic principles are usually listed in basic design books as balance, scale, proportion, rhythm, contrast, dominance, and unity. It is beyond the scope of this book to give a detailed analysis of design, nor is it necessary, since there is hardly a person today who, if interested in flower arrangement, does not instinctively or otherwise know how to design. Far more useful, in our opinion, is information on the techniques to apply to achieve the hoped-for result.

BASIC SHAPES

Most flower arrangements adhere to one of the basic shapes illustrated by the sketches on page 176. (An exception must be made for modern "free form" which has recently come into vogue at flower shows.) After deciding where the arrangement will be used, select a shape to fit the place. There is a wide choice.

FAN

SYMMETRICAL

HORIZONTAL

CONVEX CURVE

PARABOLIC ARC

Drawing 11.

THE TRIANGLE

Sketch 11 illustrates symmetrical balance. The design is capable of being divided into two similar halves by a vertical line. Other examples of the symmetrical triangle may be seen in Plates 13 and 29.

Japanese floral art is also based on the triangle, not an equilateral one, but a scalene. All sides are unequal to represent the three main elements in life—heaven, man, and earth. The disciplining line of the Japanese arrangement is the longest one. Reaching upward to represent heaven, it must be one and one-half times the height of a tall container or the width of a low one. The secondary line, man, is two-thirds as long as the heaven line, leaning away from it at an angle of twenty-five to thirty degrees. Earth, the lowest line, is about one-third the height of the heaven line and leans at about forty-five degrees. Between these basic lines, intervening lines called helpers may be used.

Drawing 12.

CRESCENT

HOGARTH

ROUND

LEFT ANGLE TRIANGLE

VERTICAL

Because of the complexity of the rules governing Japanese ways with flowers, it is the custom in America to use the general courteous term "in the oriental manner" for arrangements based on heaven-man-earth lines but not adhering to the philosophy and symbolism which underline Ikebana. See Plate 70.

LEFT-ANGLE AND RIGHT-ANGLE TRIANGLES

The left-angle and right-angle triangles give wide scope to the asymmetrical form. Plate 8 and Sketch 12 illustrate a right-angle triangle.

HALF-CIRCLE
In Sketch 11 we see the half-circle or convex curve. It is useful whenever a low arrangement is desirable, as for dining- and coffee-table decoration. See Plates 16 and 18.

THE FAN
The fan is a favorite shape for many pulpit decorations. Pulpits, being large, need full arrangements. Plate 39 exemplifies the fan shape used in the temple, and it is further illustrated by Sketch 11.

THE OVAL
This interesting shape is often used for traditional styles; it is illustrated by Color Plate I.

HOGARTH CURVE
The S-curve, or the Hogarth line of beauty, named by the English artist in the eighteenth century, is frequently used because of its grace and rhythm. Plate 94 and 98, and Sketches 8, 9 and 12 are examples of its use.

THE ROUND
The round, or circular, or full circle shape is pleasing to the eye, but care must be taken to avoid monotony. Break the outline with some foliage or use an accessory as in Plate 63.

The Vertical

A vertical shape is aspiring—it leads the eye upward, and is therefore useful in religious observance. Also it is becoming increasingly popular in our space age. The artist's Sketch 12 and Plate 32 are good examples of this form. Knowledgeable arrangers speak more and more often of line (as distinct from mass) and we see it, of course, most explicitly in the vertical shape.

The Crescent

The crescent is pleasing because the imagination stretches the lines until the complete circle is formed. The complete circle is considered natural; therefore, the crescent takes on the feel of daring, of moving away from the norm, and so, is frequently described as "advanced" and "original." See Color Plate IV, Plates 5 and 31, and Sketches 7 and 12.

The Parabolic Arc

The parabolic arc is now coming into favor. An example is seen in Plate 77 and also in Sketches 5, 6 and 11. There are two basic lines in the parabola arc and within and around these dominant lines the arrangement is created. The ends *never* meet; they are meant to stretch to infinity.

MECHANICS

The dictionary definition for mechanics is "the science of machinery," which means the way something is done. Thus, flower arranging, like anything else, must have a *way* of being accomplished. What is needed?

Tools

Whether you are making a centerpiece for a festival table or a decoration for home or sanctuary, there are certain basic needs: containers, needlepoint holders, Oasis, chicken wire, styrofoam, wire, floral and masking tape, clay and mortite, hammer, dowel sticks, tubes, bases and stands, and accessories.

CONTAINERS

Containers may be many and diversified, but they must be functional. They may vary from a flat low bowl to a tall vase, a round vegetable dish or even a long loaf pan, depending on the use. Note Plate 87 where the flower arrangement and containers are kept low. Contrast this with Plate 30, where the arrangement is above the eye level of guests so as not to impair conversation or vision.

If the arrangement is for a buffet table, any size or shape, such as a pillow vase, classic urn or pedestal, may be used. Containers need not be conventional in appearance. A piece of driftwood, a rock or pieces of metal of interesting shape, ceramic, glass or wood—all are possible. When using driftwood as a container, it is well to hollow it out to have a hole for pinholder and water. Many people enjoy using their ingenuity in the making of original containers.

HOLDERS

Needlepoint. A needlepoint holder consists of a series of small needles anchored to a base. Some holders have sides which form a cup around the needles to hold water. A cup holder is used in a container such as alabaster which might be ruined by water, or it may be used by itself as with a piece of driftwood. The needlepoint holder must be large enough to hold all the materials firmly in place. The holder should be concealed (use a large loaf, rocks, etc.) when the arrangement is finished.

Floral Clay. The holder may be secured to the bottom of a flat container by waterproof floral clay or mortite.

Drawing 13.

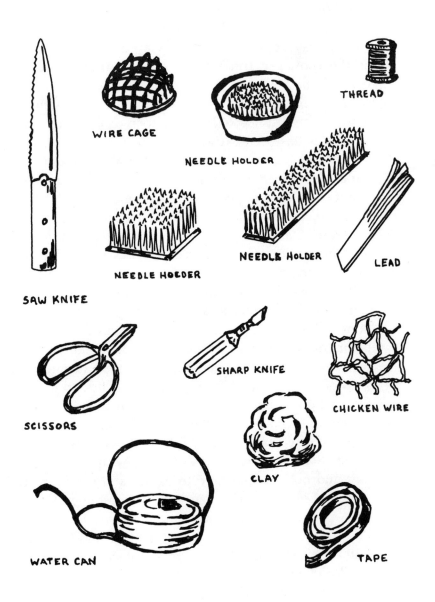

THREAD

WIRE CAGE

NEEDLE HOLDER

NEEDLE HOLDER

NEEDLE HOLDER

LEAD

SAW KNIFE

SCISSORS

SHARP KNIFE

CHICKEN WIRE

CLAY

WATER CAN

TAPE

Drawing 14.

Be sure container, holder and clay are absolutely dry; then roll a piece of clay between the hands until it forms a long roll. Place the roll on the bottom outside edge of the holder all the way around. Place the clayed side on the surface of the container and press firmly, securing the clay and needlepoint holder to the container.

Paraffin. If a container is too tall for plant stems, pack it first with crushed, wet newspaper, from which most of the water has been extracted. Push paper down as tightly as possible; on top of that put several thicknesses of dry paper. Now melt paraffin and pour it into the container, about one-eighth to one-fourth of an inch thick. Then lower the needlepoint holder into the melted paraffin, and let set.

Oasis. Oasis is a plastic sponge-like material that comes in round or brick shape. It is easily cut with a table knife to the required size. It is wise to have the block extend several inches above the top of the container, so flowers and foliage can be added on the sides as well as hanging over the container. Soak the Oasis in a pan for a half hour to an hour before using so that it absorbs its maximum amount of water. Place it in the container and tape it down with a strip of floral or masking tape attached first to one side of the container, then carried over the top of the Oasis and on to the other side. This secures the Oasis. Do this twice in opposite directions. Oasis will hold the material and retain water. Soak the Oasis a third time, wrap it in aluminum foil, and poke holes where the flowers are to be placed.

Chicken Wire. Chicken wire is most useful for large urns, pitchers and deep containers holding heavy material. Push or punch the chicken wire together and force into the container. After the flowers are in place, add water.

Styrofoam. This is a hard white plastic that does not hold water; it comes in sheets, one and two inches thick, and in various shapes such as cones and balls. It is perfect for dried and permanent arrangements. The cones and balls are excellent for topiary trees. Styrofoam must be cut with a sharp knife or a saw. Insert it in the container and tape in place. It may also be used by itself. Cut a hole into it for a cup holder with fresh material. This material will hold arrangements very well. Since styrofoam does not require water, it should last indefinitely.

Clippers. Clippers are essential. They come in different sizes and shapes. One kind has a short squat handle and tip; it is good for woody material, branches, thick stems, etc. The other style has a long handle and corresponding nose and is perfect for the more delicately stemmed material.

Scissors. Use scissors for trimming tape or a leaf which is perfect in line but slightly brown on the edges; trim the telltale brown away with scissors.

Hammer. Pound woody stems before putting them in water. This allows for maximum absorption and the material will remain in good condition for a reasonable length of time.

Wire. Wire has many uses. Here are five suggestions: 1. When working with a bud or a short flower, fill a small orchid tube with water, put on its cover, which has a hole in the top, and then insert the flower into the tube. Next, wire the tube to a dowel stick, a woody stem or the like; the bud or flower may then be placed at any desired point. 2. When working with broad-leaved foliage, if an unusual curve is desired or if the heavy leaf will not stay with just gentle hand bending, cut a piece of wire and tape it with Scotch tape to the back of the leaf. Then bend the leaf into the desired curve; it will hold. 3. Wire or tape may also be used when a stem is not thick enough for the needles of a needlepoint holder. Take a thick stem or branch and wire or tape the thin stem to it at the bottom; it is then thick enough to be placed where necessary. 4. Wire is useful too when attaching grapes in an arrangement. String the wire through the top of the grapes (the stem) and then onto a small dowel stick to be inserted onto the needlepoint holder or into the Oasis.

5. To wire nuts (as used in Plate 24) drill a hole through end, put a piece of wire through hole, and wire several nuts together to form a bunch. Handle like grapes.

Bases. A base is a finishing touch. It elevates an arrangement, and sets it off. Select the base to harmonize with the container and setting. There are round, square and rectangular bases of varying thicknesses, sizes, and substances—everything from highly polished formal teakwood to rough-hewn stone. Free form bases may be purchased or made from plywood. They are effective when incorporating figures, driftwood, etc., in arrangements. It is wise to have several shapes on hand and to experiment with them to see which base is best suited.

Accessories. An accessory is that extra something which completes a design. In Plate 59, an Arbor Day table, the use of the figure of a man planting his tree, adds realism. Plate 82 makes an extremely original use of a Torah crown as an accessory, and has a direct line of communication to the festival of *Shabuoth.* Color Plate IV, for a *Bar Mitzvah* reception table, effectively uses a piece of contemporary sculpture, the Rabbi holding aloft the Torah, which has so much significance for the *Bar Mitzvah* ceremony. Except for the explicit symbol of the particular festival, Judaism permits a limited use of statues and figures. For this reason, we welcome them in flower decorations which have social rather than spiritual meaning.

CONDITIONING OF FLOWERS

All cut flowers need water. They will soak up their maximum need if the needlepoint holders and containers are kept clean and if the cutting tools are very sharp. All flowers, whether cut from the garden or bought at the florist's, must immediately be placed deep in warm water so stems are fully immersed. They should be kept for at least two hours before they are used.

The stems of some plants will "bleed" when cut—dahlias, poinsettias, poppies, hollyhocks and ferns. Instead of cutting these flowers, burn the ends and plunge them immediately into water for several hours before using. Heavy, woody stems should be hammered at the bottom so that they absorb a maximum amount of water. Lilacs should have their stems hammered and the flowers completely submerged in water for two hours. All soft leaves should be completely submerged for two hours for proper conditioning. If leaves are ragged or unattractive, strip them off and use only the flowers.

Most arrangers like to cut stems at a slant rather than straight across to provide a larger surface for water intake.

DRYING FLOWERS AND FOLIAGE

Drying flowers and foliage involves a bit of effort, but has its compensations. It may lead to a pleasant hobby and throughout the winter the home will be brightened with colorful bouquets.

Drying Flowers. Most of the summer garden flowers may be dried in the following way. Use white sand alone, or make a mixture of white sand and about one-eighth to one-fourth of borax. Sift the mixture and put about two inches of it in a receptable such as a shoe box. Lay the flowers, stems up, a few inches apart on the sand; with a spoon, carefully work in more of the mixture around all petals until the flowers are entirely covered. For successful results both sand and flowers must be dry at the beginning. The mixture may be sifted and used numerous times. Smaller, dainty flowers may be inserted later and the process may be continued. Label and date. After two or three weeks remove the mixture gradually and lift out the flowers carefully.

Silica gel, available under various brand names, is excellent for drying flowers to preserve their color. Follow manufacturer's directions.

Many flowers, such as yarrow, celosia (cockscomb), Chinese lanterns, lunaria (honesty), and strawflowers dry very well if hung upside down in bunches in a dry, airy place.

Preserving Foliage. Foliage may be preserved in a solution of glycerine (⅓) and water (⅔) or in an anti-freeze such as Prestone. Place the leaves (after pounding the stems two inches at the bottom) in a tall narrow bottle containing four to six inches of the solution. Let them remain for two or three weeks. Early fall is the best time for drying foliage.

Pine cones, seed pods, ferns, grains and driftwood may be used effectively in dried arrangements.

Photograph Credits

Adams, Eugene, Pittsburgh, Pa.: #112; Allen, William, New Canaan, Conn.: #57; Burns, Sheldon, Altoona, Pa.: #6; Bramore Studio, Rockaway Park, N. Y.: #15, 35, 44; Cardell, Pittsburgh, Pa.: #103; Chick, Robert, Rochester, N. Y.: #49, 53, 96; Coe, Daniel, Cleveland, Ohio: #31; Dallinger, Herbert, Los Angeles, Calif.: #67, 90; Demeree, Ralph, San Francisco, Calif.: #16, 71; Field, White Plains, N. Y.: #3; Genereux, Paul, Lynn, Mass.: #17, 85, 91; Jonas Studio, Inc., Pittsburgh, Pa.: #100, 101, 102, 104, 105, 106, 107, 108, 109, 110; Kaufman, Pittsburgh, Pa.: Color Plate I; Kuhn, Robert L., Los Angeles, Calif.: #18; Latent Image: S. William Hinzman, Pittsburgh, Pa.: Jacket Plate,Color Plate II, III, IV; #1, 2, 5, 7, 9, 10, 11, 12, 13, 14, 19, 20, 21, 22, 23, 24, 25, 27, 28, 29, 30, 34, 36, 37, 43, 45, 46, 47, 48, 50, 51, 52, 55, 56, 59, 60, 61, 62, 63, 65, 66, 68, 69, 70, 72, 73, 74, 81, 82, 83, 84, 86, 88, 92, 93, 94, 97, 98, 99, 111; Latent Image: Russell W. Streiner and George A. Romero, Pittsburgh, Pa.: #75, 76, 77, 80; Linsey, Martin, Shaker Heights, Ohio: #64, 87; Markow, Jack, and Company, Ltd., Montreal, Canada: #33; Meyers, Ralph J., Cleveland, Ohio: #32; Miller, Sam, Philadelphia, Pa.: #40; Pomeroy Studio, New Rochelle, N. Y.: #26; Rinkel, Harry, San Francisco, Calif.: #8, 54; Savler, David, Montgomery, Ala.: #42; Schnellbacher, Elton, Pittsburgh, Pa.: #4; St. Petersburg Times Commercial Photographic Department, St. Petersburg, Fla.: #89; Wakelin, John K., Toledo, Ohio: #41, 78; Whitestone, New York, N. Y.: #79.

Bibliography

Agnon, S. Y. *Days of Awe.* New York: Schocken Books, 1948.

Askwith, Herbert (ed.), Meikle, Catherine E. (ass't.), *The Complete Guide to Garden Flowers.* New York: A. S. Barnes & Co., 1961.

Benz, M. *Flowers: Free Form—Interpretive Design.* Houston: San Jacinto Publishing Co., 1960.

Clements, Julia. *Floral Roundabout.* London: C. Arthur Pearson Ltd., 1950.

———. *Fun With Flowers.* London: C. Arthur Pearson Ltd., 1950.

———. *Party Pieces.* London: C. Arthur Pearson Ltd., 1950.

Conway, J. Gregory. *Encyclopedia of Flower Arranging.* New York: Alfred A. Knopf Inc., 1959.

———. *Flower Arranging Through the Year.* New York: Alfred A. Knopf Inc., 1957.

———. *Flowers East-West.* New York: Alfred A. Knopf Inc., 1948.

———. *Flowers, Their Arrangement.* New York: Alfred A. Knopf Inc., 1940.

Cusin, Silvio G. *Art in the Jewish Tradition.* Milan: Adei-Wizo, 1963.

Cyphers, Emma Hodkinson. *Modern Art in Flower Arrangement.* New York: Hearthside Press Inc., 1959.

Eichholz, Georg. *Landscapes of the Bible.* transl. by John W. Doberstein. New York: Harper & Row, 1963.

Foley, Daniel J. *Garden Flowers in Color.* New York: Macmillan Co., 1949.

Freehof, Solomon B. *Home Friday Evening Service.* (leaflet) Rodef Shalom Temple, Pittsburgh, 1934.

———. *The Small Sanctuary.* (Judaism in the Prayerbook.) Union of American Hebrew Congregations, Cincinnati, 1942.

Ginzberg, Louis. *The Legends of the Jews.* Vols. I-VII, Philadelphia: Jewish Publication Society of America, 1913.

Goldson, Rae L. *Contemporary Flower Arrangement.* New York: Hearthside Press Inc., 1955.

————. *Contemporary Flower Arrangement.* New York: Hearthside Press Inc., 1955, revised, 1962.

Greenberg, Betty D. and Silverman, Altheo O. *The Jewish Home Beautiful.* The National Women's League of the United Synagogue of America, New York, 1958.

Hill, Amelia Leavitt. *The Complete Book of Table Setting and Flower Arrangements.* London: Greystone Press, 1949.

Hirsch, Sylvia. *The Art of Table Setting and Flower Arrangement.* New York: Crowell Co., 1962.

Ishimoto, Tatsuo. *The Art of Driftwood and Dried Arrangements.* New York: Crown Publishers Inc., 1951.

Mullins, Ruth E. *Religious Themes in Flower Arrangements.* New York: Hearthside Press, 1959.

Perry, Francis. *The Woman Gardener.* New York: Farrar, Strauss & Cudahy, 1955.

Roberts, Patricia Easterbrook. *Flower Arrangements Through the Year.* London: Thames & Hudson, 1963.

————. *Simplified Flower Arrangements.* New York: Viking Press Inc., 1960.

Rockwell, F. F., and Grayson, Esther C. *The Complete Book of Flower Arrangement.* Doubleday & Co. Inc., 1948.

Rosenau, William. *Jewish Ceremonial Institutions and Customs.* New York: Bloch Publishing, 1925.

Schauss, Hayyim. *The Jewish Festivals.* Union of American Hebrew Congregations, New York, 1938.

Schulke, Zelda Wyatt. *Holiday and Party Table Settings.* New York: Hearthside Press Inc., 1960.

Singer. (translator). *The Authorized Daily Prayerbook.* London: Eyre and Spottiswoode, 1912.

Spry, Constance. *Party Flowers.* London: J. D. Dent & Sons Ltd., 1955.

Taylor, Norman. *The Practical Encyclopedia of Gardening in Dictionary Form.* Garden City, N. Y., 1936.

Walker, Winifred. *All the Plants of the Bible.* New York: Harper & Brothers, 1957.

Wilson, Helen Van Pelt. *Flower Arrangements; Designs for Today.* Princeton: D. Van Nostrand Co., Inc., 1962.

Wilson, Lois. *Miniature Flower Arrangements and Plantings.* Princeton: D. Van Nostrand Co., Inc., 1963.

Zangwill, Israel. (translator). "The Feast of the Law," in *The Service of the Synagogue.* (6 vols.). London: George Routledge & Sons, Ltd., 1908.

"Flower Arranging," in *Better Homes and Gardens.* New York: Meredith Publishing Co., 1957.

The Jewish Encyclopedia. New York, London: Funk and Wagnalls Co., 1905.

The Universal Jewish Encyclopedia. New York: The Universal Jewish Encyclopedia Inc., 1940.

Index